Educating For a New Millennium

Views of 132 International Scholars

by

Harold G. Shane
Indiana University, Bloomington

with

M. Bernadine Tabler
Indiana University, New Albany

A Diamond Jubilee Publication of the
Phi Delta Kappa Educational Foundation
Bloomington, Indiana

Cover design by Victoria Voelker

Library of Congress Catalogue Card Number 81-82883
ISBN 0-87367-775-1
Printed in the United States of America

For Kate

Contents

Figures

Foreword

For a number of years Americans have been interested in what the future holds for them. Recognizing the importance of tomorrow's world for today's youth, Phi Delta Kappa requested funding from the Lilly Endowment in Indianapolis to conduct a future-focused study of education as a part of its Diamond Jubilee celebration in 1981.

The idea behind the study was a simple one: What do distinguished international scholars in the natural and social sciences identify as concepts in their fields of expertise that young persons should understand if they are to survive the troubled years that lie ahead? Also, what do they need to learn in order to live more humanely with their fellow citizens?

With funding from the Lilly Endowment, the PDK inquiry was begun in 1980 under the direction of Harold G. Shane for whom Indiana University provided a leave of absence. By the fall of 1981 he and the project staff had interviewed 132 scholars following procedures described in Appendix A, and had begun work on the manuscript.

Even before its publication, preliminary reports on the study created international interest. I hope that Kappans and other educators will find the survival concepts identified by the scholars as provocative as I did!

On behalf of Phi Delta Kappa, I wish to thank the Lilly Endowment for its continued interest in and support for education, and to express appreciation to Indiana University for contributing Dr. Shane's services.

Lowell C. Rose
Executive Secretary
Phi Delta Kappa

Preface

A great many people gave generously of their time and effort before and during the Phi Delta Kappa Diamond Jubilee Project which eventuated in *Educating for a New Millennium*. Lowell C. Rose, PDK executive secretary, and Stanley M. Elam, PDK director of publications, were important sources of ideas while the study was being planned. Dean Evans, senior project officer for the Lilly Endowment, encouraged our efforts and supported the grant request, which funded the travel and other costs involved in our 132 international interviews.

Our preliminary planning group of executive officers of professional associations and specialists in futures studies, who are identified in Appendix A, were generous with their time and exceedingly helpful with their advice. Appreciation also is due to the U.S. chaired professors, senior university administrators, and scholars overseas who helped us choose a panel of distinguished natural and social scientists to interview for this study. Special thanks are due Eleonora Masini of the Pontifical Gregoriana University in Rome for arranging interviews in Spain, France, and Italy; and to Lord Perry, head of Britain's Open University, who helped us identify scholars at distinguished institutions in the United Kingdom. Malcolm Mackenzie of the University of Glasgow also was most kind in arranging a round of interviews in Scotland.

Gary Sojka, chairman of the Department of Biology at Indiana University, was generous with his time in making suggestions from a scientist's point of view to improve chapters 3 and 4. Excellent editorial suggestions also were made by Stanley M. Elam. Another PDK staff member, Willard Duckett, helped prepare our grant request to the Lilly Endowment, provided wise counsel, and subsequently handled the disbursement of funds with promptness and efficiency.

Extensive work on the manuscript and graphics was done by Derek L. Burleson, editor of special publications for Phi Delta Kappa. Not only was he marvelously helpful on ideas and on details, I am especially appreciative of his forbearance and understanding when our original deadline had to be extended because the scholarly group ultimately interviewed was much larger than the 50 persons originally contemplated.

Deeply involved in the day-to-day work that went into our report were M. Bernadine Tabler, project associate; Anne Ingram Merkel, project assistant; and Velma Trussell, senior project secretary and editorial assistant. A highly qualified teacher, Mrs. Trussell was invaluable for her advice, managerial skills, and memory for details. Original art work by Diane Jung was important in clarifying ideas in the text.

Dr. Tabler and Miss Merkel crisscrossed the U.S. for interviews on the East and West coasts plus points between. Dr. Tabler also participated in initial planning and completed a round of interviews in England. Once the field work had been done, she wrote first drafts of chapters 7 and 8 and edited the entire manuscript. Sue Logsdon, who expertly typed and retyped portions of the manuscript, assisted us in making many deadlines.

Lastly, and most important was the consistent help from my wife, Catherine McKenzie Shane. Her editorial work was invaluable and, in Europe, her bilingual skills were important to the success of a number of our interviews.

Harold G. Shane
April 1981

I

Concepts for Survival: The Views of 132 Scholars in the Natural and Social Sciences

1

How Shall We Educate for a New Millennium?

Prepared by 13 agencies of the federal government including the Central Intelligence Agency (CIA) and the Department of Agriculture, the Global 2000 Report *projected a world population of 6.35 billion in the year 2000 (up from 4 billion in 1975), a Mexico City swollen to 31 million, and at least five other cities with from 15 to 20 million inhabitants (Calcutta, Bombay, Cairo, Jakarta, and Seoul). Malnourished humans presumably will top 1.3 billion, with uncounted children dead or mentally and physically stunted 20 years hence by the ravages of hunger. Increasing shortages and such environmental horrors as acid rain, more pesticide-resistant insects, and a 33% increase in the volume of carbon dioxide are anticipated, and no prospect of "quick fixes" is foreseen.*

—Global 2000 Report

In the present context of global conflict, terrorism, and hunger—as reflected in the statements above and as recorded daily by the media—it makes sense to ask whether U.S. schools need to make substantial changes; and more important, should we modify our present curricular and instructional practices? This was the query we directed to 132 internationally respected scholars in the natural and the social sciences whom we interviewed for this study. Their responses provided the data base for this monograph.[1]

What images of the probable world of the future should shape our planning? What are the implications of contemporary developments in science, technology, and world societies for curriculum development and instructional practices?[2] Our responses to these questions

[1]As a part of its Diamond Jubilee activities in 1981, Phi Delta Kappa planned and carried out the study reported here with funding from the Lilly Endowment. The 132 natural and social scientists interviewed and their institutional affiliations are identified in Appendix B.

[2]The procedures followed in our inquiry are presented in Appendix A.

are based on the survival skills and desirable personal qualities proposed by our scholarly panel.

Learning in a New Millennium

The crucial years: 1986-2006. As one examines the literature produced since the mid-1950s, it becomes evident that a few wise, perceptive men and women provided us with early warnings about the many problems and the increasingly frequent crisis that began to surface during the 1970s and which seem certain to trouble us during the remaining years of this century.[3] Various events of the past decade, of which the continuing energy deficit is a costly reminder, have made it clear that the 25 years between 1981 and 2006 will be crucial. The first five to 10 years of this interval may well present some of the most important social decisions ever to face the U.S. and other nations. The two decades between 1986 and 2006 probably will prove to be even more portentous, because it is during this period that humans will need to implement choices that are necessary to ward off potential catastrophies which, as chapter 2 will make clear, greatly disturb many of the scientists we interviewed.

The extent of the challenge to the world's people was expressed both bluntly and succinctly by panelist Aurelio Peccei, co-founder of the Club of Rome:

> Ten years ago, we at the Club of Rome predicted that bad social management, the wasting of resources, widespread pollution, and rapid overpopulation would eventually strangle civilization. We now have increasing violence, fewer energy resources, military buildups, more economic difficulties, and continuing overpopulation. . . . Today the world begins more and more to resemble a ricocheting bullet as it careens from disaster to disaster.[4]

Comparable statements are abundant and come from many of our best informed thinkers, but judging by the recent course of events, most of their messages have yet to get a foothold. Fortunately, there is some lead time for planning—perhaps five to 10 years—and with luck, about 20 years more in which to begin to attack global problems. Unless present trends are reversed, irreparable damage is likely to be done to the biosphere by exploitation of nonrenewable re-

---

[3]One of the most prescient was Sir Geoffrey Vickers whose beautifully written expressions of concern date back at least to 1954. Rachel Carson's *The Silent Spring*, written in the early 1960s, and the Club of Rome reports such as *The Limits to Growth* and *Mankind at the Turning Point*, which appeared during the 1970s, are well-known benchmark publications warning of possible ecocatastrophies.

[4]Aurelio Peccei, "The Challenge of the 80's," in Frank Feather, ed. *Through the '80s* (Washington, D.C.: World Future Society, 1980), p. 430.

sources, by pollution, by nuclear war, or by unchecked human reproduction. Education on a worldwide scale for the young and for adults becomes more significant with every passing day. Whatever differences there were in their images of the future among the scholars with whom we consulted, there was general agreement that an educated, informed, world citizenry has become consumately important.

Schooling, education, and learning. For purposes of clarity, let us define the terms *schooling, education,* and *learning,* since curriculum planning is influenced by the connotations ascribed to each of these terms.

Schooling, for our purposes, refers to a program of planned and organized instruction that is intended to maintain and to enhance one's sense of identity. Schooling is designed to transmit and to preserve in the young those skills, attitudes, and values that are prized by their elders and that are deemed to be essential to the community's well-being. Traditionally, schooling has been designed predominantly for children and youth.

Education, as we define it, has a much broader connotation than schooling. It is associated with a wider age range as indicated by our frequent use of such terms as "adult education," "mature learners," and "continuing education." It also includes learning from many out-of-school or paracurricular[5] experiences—often in the world of work—that seem likely to eventuate in improved ways of behaving.

Learning, in our definition, transcends both schooling and education. It involves those lifelong exposures that change behavior to create the personal attributes and qualities that make each individual unique: knowledge, values, ways of thinking and acting, skills, and so on, acquired from participation in lifelong living and learning.

Curriculum content in and for the future, we believe, should permeate all three—schooling, education, and learning. It is our hope that the present study will shed considerable light on the question of what subject matter, attitudes, and understandings promise to help learners, both the young and the mature, not only to survive the vicissitudes of years to come, but also to contribute their talents and their time to making tomorrow work.

Since school children of the Eighties and Nineties will not yet be in the seats of power in government, business, industry, labor, or the media, the concepts suggested by our panel of scholars are of equal or greater importance to today's adults. They also must be "learning for

---

[5]The term *paracurriculum* refers to the body of out-of-school experience that helps to strengthen the learner's intellectual ability, general background and coping powers.

a new millennium" in order to engage in wise decision making necessary to, first, contain the impending world chaos and, second, bring about those changes which Barbara Ward describes as "progress for a small planet."

Complexities of Curriculum Planning for Tomorrow's World

Most parents and teachers probably would not dispute humanistic scientist John Platt's point that the world presently is passing through the greatest evolutionary jump in its history.[6] He tells us that since 1940 we have had more wrenching changes occur than in the previous 600 years! Molecular biology, recombinant DNA, nuclear power, moon landings, jet propulsion, television, electronic data processing, and systems analysis are among some of the more spectacular developments.

The curriculum changes and innovations that are most suitable to so dynamic an era are much more open to dispute. As the 1970s unrolled, there was vehement debate over such developments as the back-to-basics movement, competency-based diplomas, Public Law 94-142 legislated on behalf of the handicapped, bilingual education, declining test scores, and affirmative action. The Eighties promise to be even more controversial as educators continue to explore better ways of helping young and old learn to cope with rapid global change, using tools that have yet to be tested.

The genesis of issues. The world of the year 2000 seems likely to be far more different from the world of 1980 than the world of 1930 was from that of 1910. Curriculum workers will be faced with a wide array of issues as they try to improve learning experiences for the young. But before we examine the roots of discord that create curriculum issues, let us comment briefly about the genesis of issues.

An issue arises when individuals or groups feel that there is a threat to their health, financial security, reputation, social status, or the general welfare of themselves and their children. In many instances it does not matter whether the threat is real or fancied; it is how people *feel* that leads to confrontations, to picket lines, and sometimes, to battle lines. In recent years attempts to deal with problems of desegregation in the U.S. illustrate how issues can become explosive.

The roots of discord. In the U.S. and throughout the world, some people are winners; others are losers. They fall respectively into

---

[6]John Platt, "The Greatest Evolutionary Jump in History," in Frank Feather, ed., *Through the 80's* (Washington, D.C.: World Future Society, 1980), pp. 12-15.

"have more" and "have less" distributions. Conjecture leads one to suspect that issues are rooted in the pressure or tension that is created when, as figure 1 suggests, those below the median seek to shift the line, become winners, and join the "have more" group as suggested by the dotted line and by the curved arrow at the left of the model. Further social and economic tension is generated, as the curved arrow on the right indicates, when some of the "have mores" become losers and are forced to enter the "have less" category.

As economist Lester C. Thurow has pointed out, while each of our problems has a theoretical solution, in practice it is difficult to make any social decisions when everyone has a direct self-interest in the outcome of such decisions! For instance, he tells us, "Every time a tax is levied or repealed, every time public expenditures are expanded or contracted, every time regulations are extended or abolished, an equity decision has to be made. Since economic gains are relatively easy to allocate, the basic problem comes down to allocating economic losses. Whose income 'ought' to go down?"[7]

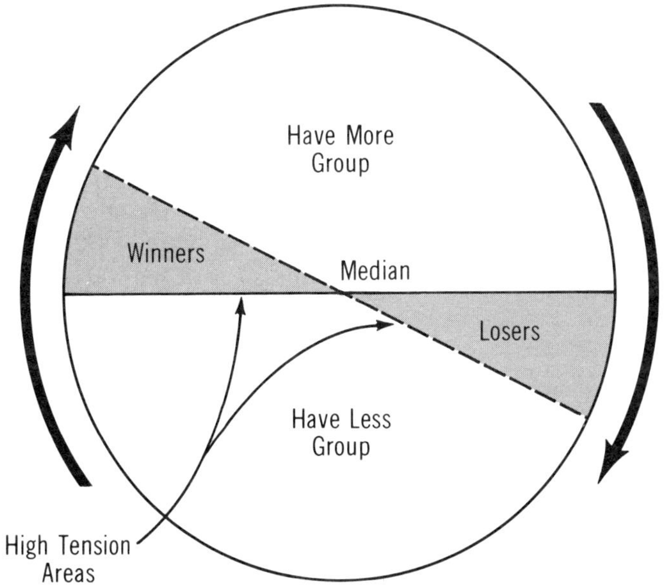

Fig. 1. Sources of potential discord

[7]Lester C. Thurow, *The Zero-Sum Society* (New York: Basic Books, Inc., 1980), p. 17.

To put it another way, many people in the U.S. really do not want equalitarian democracy. They see democracy as a social order which provides opportunity for upward mobility and privilege. They seek equality with the top 10% with respect to socioeconomic status. This tacit rejection of equalitarian economic democracy creates a quandary for curriculum planners. How does one plan for a turbulent future when, both nationally and globally, there is such great potential for discord growing out of conflicting self-interests?

The Curriculum Planner's Quandary: Which Future World Will We Choose?

The harsh social decisions facing our society are not only problems of overpopulation, pollution, or resource depletion. We have reduced the U.S. birthrate, have begun to reduce pollution, and are beginning to protect our nonrenewable resources. The real dilemma is that almost everyone wants to get more than they have, as suggested by figure 1. This situation requires some elaboration and explanation since it is likely to worsen in the next 20 years.

By the early 1980s most informed Americans were beginning to realize that a contraction of material wealth was occurring and that there was a need for greater frugality. As one of our panelists, psychobiologist W. Jackson Davis, phrased it:

> I think we will move forward, not backward, into a simpler life. We are going to face the future without [as much] energy, but with a population that has been generated by energy. If we don't change our values, then the depletion of energy and resources will do it for us.

The interviews with our other panelists suggest that few scientists would dispute Davis' statement. However, the question of *who* will determine the nature of economic redistribution policies is quite another matter! Consider the statement made by Torsten Husén of the University of Stockholm: "The key concept in the controversies permeating the highly industrial and postindustrial societies is equality, both as it is interpreted philosophically and the way it is translated into social action. Does it mean equality of *opportunity* or equality of *results*?"

Economics professor Fritz Machlup at Princeton gave one answer to Husén's question. He contended that equality of income and wealth was an impossible dream for the world's societies. British sociologist Tessa Blackstone, on the other hand, insisted that students must learn that there is a need to redistribute the world's goods because of the large inequalities between and within industrialized and underdeveloped societies.

The opinions of our panelists cited above illustrate the quandary in which educators, especially social studies teachers and curriculum workers, find themselves. How does one determine the kind of world, in terms of politics, economics, social policies, and uses of technology, that is the most desirable one for us to seek? And what educational strategies will be most effective in creating this world and at the same time strengthen American-style democracy? The task of defining the sort of world in which "liberty and justice for all" prevails should be shared by all citizens. It will be a long, hard task marked by conflicting opinions and many confrontations.

Educators responsible for the climate of learning in our schools are charged with the unique and challenging task of developing and revising curriculum content in a time of turbulence. Therefore we hope that this inventory of basic concepts for coping with the future will prove useful as curriculum content and for sharpening educators' societal insights as well.

The spectrum of choices before us. We will present and interpret six options, any one of which might serve as a value base for curriculum development. However, we will not reveal until the final chapter which ones our interview data suggest are most promising. The next three chapters present the concepts our panel of scientists believe students need to grasp; and the following four chapters explore the curriculum content and changes in instructional practice that our inquiry seems to support. The final chapter provides a summary and recommendations.

The six alternative approaches to curriculum planning that we have selected are:

1. The regressive option—return to some of the values and practices that have been discarded.

2. The conservative option—leave things as they are.

3. The liberal option—adopt changes that are mandated by a changing society.

4. The experimental option—create new educational designs.

5. The regenerative option—adopt new approaches to learning experiences.

6. The eclectic option—any one or any combination of the above might be the best option.

The regressive option is based on the assumption that discipline and intellectual rigor, which will be required for the future, have deteriorated and that cognitive development has been superseded by a concern for social and affective development. Furthermore, motivation has been lost because "hard" subject matter and competitive grading have been replaced by equalitarian, life-adjustment programs where presumably everyone is a winner. One outcome has been impairment in the quality of secondary education, as reflected in declining test scores. Colleges have, as a result, become less intellectual in their emphases.

The regressive option would seek to restore the high standards associated with an intellectually elitist era, which prevailed in the British grammar schools of yesteryear or in U.S. private schools, where programs were rigidly determined by college admission requirements. Its proponents argue that the projected outcome of this option would be a higher output of persons prepared to cope with tomorrow because of their substantive knowledge and leadership abilities.

The conservative option is designed to preserve those qualities that its supporters suggest are the best of present instructional practices—"to try nothing for the first time." Also included in this option is the continuing quest for basic literacy skills. The major difference between the regressive and the conservative positions is that the former stresses an elitist approach while the latter emphasizes basic education for all.

The liberal option is sometimes accused by its critics of deemphasizing academic content. However, its proponents stress practices that improve the performance of all learners by recognizing individual differences, psychosocial needs, and meaningful learning. Advocates of liberal option education often tend to utilize innovative and sometimes untested practices.

The experimental option, in addition to accepting liberal option practices, encourages the creation and validation of novel approaches to the improvement of teaching and learning, attempts to design curriculum around real world needs, and seeks to bring about certain social reforms to assure equitable educational opportunity.

The advocates of both liberal and experimental approaches tend to reject the elitist and competitive stance of the regressive option as well as the "status quo policy" of the conservatives. Instead, they methodically seek new or promising ideas and endeavor to generate and implement experimental or innovative practices.

The regenerative option is concerned with radical change. The term implies a substantial reform or reestablishment of educational practices and learning experiences. While advocates of the liberal and experimental options are likely to conceptualize good education as today's education with its problems removed, the proponents of the

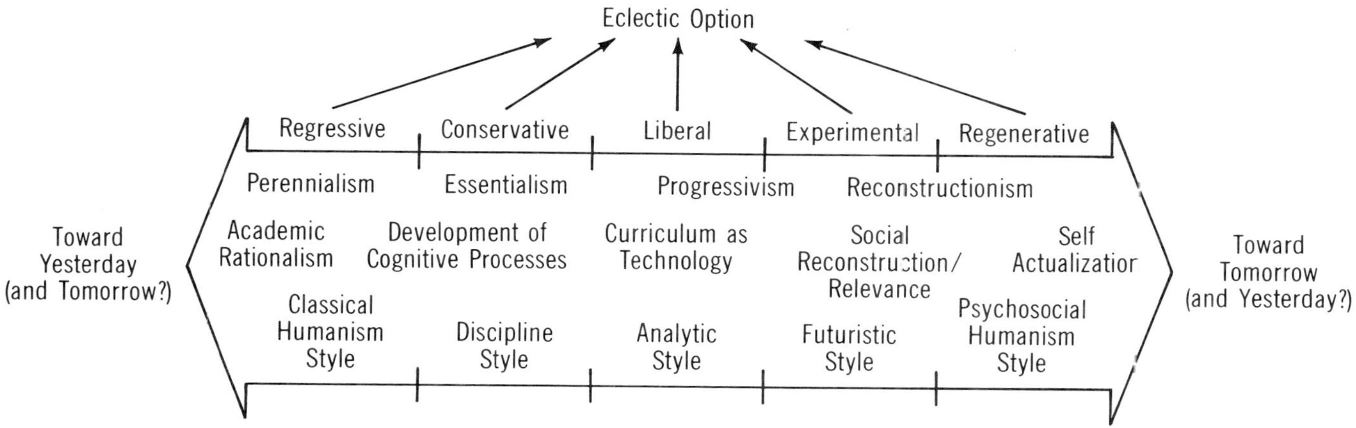

Fig. 2. The taxonomy of curriculum options

Theodore Brameld identified the following options some 30 years ago: 1) perennialism, to designate those who see "perenially contemporary" values in the cultural heritage (e.g., Robert M. Hutchins, Mortimer Adler, Stringfellow Barr); 2) essentialism, which emphasizes basic education (e.g., William Bagley, Henry C. Morrison, Arthur Bestor); 3) progressivism, to label the early proponents of open education (e.g., Carleton W. Washburne); and 4) reconstructionism, which considers schooling as a means of developing a "new social order" (e.g., George S. Counts, Theodore Brameld, and more recently such prophets of reform as Ivan Illich.)

Elliot Eisner and Elizabeth Vallance (1974) use the following terms to distinguish conflicting curriculum conceptions: 1) academic rationalism, 2) development of cognitive processes, 3) curriculum as technology, 4) social reconstruction/relevance, and 5) self-actualization/consummatory experience.

Donald E. Orlosky and B. Othanel Smith (1978) use the following terms: 1) the classical humanism style, 2) the discipline style, 3) the analytic style, and 4) the futuristic style, and psychosocial humanism style (associated with Abraham H. Maslow and Carl Rogers).

regenerative option see education for the future in radically new or different forms.

The eclectic option selects a combination of various doctrines, beliefs, or practices, depending on the age of the learners, their individual differences, the subject matter, or the socioeconomic and cultural backgrounds of the group. Thus, in a given situation, it is conceivable that an eclectic option might comprise aspects of regressive, experimental, and regenerative practices! Such a blending of seemingly contradictory options is actually consistent, according to its proponents, because an eclectic approach inherently involves selecting what appears likely to comprise the best combination.

Curriculum literature is rife with in-group terminology. Figure 2 and its accompanying notes are intended to clarify the curriculum options in the form of a taxonomic chart that compares the above classification with three additional classifications by well known persons in the field of curriculum theory.

This summary of curriculum options is offered to help educators extend their thinking about curriculum change and to begin thinking in terms of appropriate options to foster better learning for living on a rapidly changing planet.

The interesting and sometime provocative, futuristic world views of the scientists involved in this study are presented in some detail in chapter 2. Chapters 3 and 4 present the basic concepts identified by natural and social scientists as being most important for survival in the future world.

The last four chapters deal with the evolutionary changes required of public education in the future and with how survival concepts might be translated into curriculum content. Then we introduce the idea of a curriculum derived from images of the future, a curriculum that anticipates tomorrow. Last, we present the implications of this anticipatory curriculum as a spectrum ranging from early childhood to old age.

2

The Tapestry of Time: 1981-2006

And new philosophy calls all in doubt,
The element of fire is quite put out;
The sun is lost, and th'earth, an no man's wit
Can well direct him where to look for it.
And freely men confess that this world's spent,
When in the planets and the firmament
They seek so many new; they see that this
Is crumbled out again to his atomies.
'Tis all in pieces, all coherence gone.
—John Donne

In Bayeux, France, hangs a famous tapestry made under the direction of Queen Matilda, wife of William the Conqueror. Designed as a gift for Odo, the local bishop, the Bayeux tapestry recounts events leading up to the Norman Conquest of England in 1066 and depicts the culminating Battle of Hastings. In the 230 feet of fabric some 20 inches wide there are 72 panels, a tapestry of time through which history is revisited.

If a latter day Matilda lived in the year 2006 and were to do a similar summary of the past 25 years, what might the tapestry portray? Some inferences about its content can be made from comments and speculations of the 132 scholars participating in our inquiry.[1]

Images of Tomorrow

Five images of tomorrow's world emerged from the replies of the

[1]Readers are reminded that the viewpoints which follow are, to some extent, extrapolated. Participants in the study were *not* explicitly asked to speculate about the future, but their responses almost invariably reflected their images of the future. See chapters 3 and 4, which preserve statements from the interviews and from correspondence.

natural and social scientists. Their ideas suggest an exciting quarter century in the making.

1. *Tomorrow as today with fewer problems.* A small minority of panelists saw the coming decade as an extension of the present, but with appropriate steps being taken to insure a better future, including a more equitable sharing of the fruits of an increasingly industrialized world. Instead of slicing the industrial "pie" of gross world production into smaller pieces, these optimists saw an enlarged production of consumer goods and social services with more widespread distribution.

2. *Scientific, technological solutions.* Closely related to the preceding group were those who had confidence in the power of the human mind not only to continue to alter the environment but to control, through reasoned scientific and technological know-how, the course of events in socially and ecologically desirable ways. The opinions of persons in this group suggested that further increases in human knowledge and in technical prowess would help insure improved global standards of living. These panelists did not speculate on the possibility that increased scientific and technological developments could also make the future world civilization even more uncontrollable and unpredictable.

3. *Return to a low energy, more labor intensive era.* The third group was less sanguine than those described above. Sir Nevill Mott, a Nobel prize winner in physics, envisioned the world of tomorrow as one in which the per capita energy available by the year 2000 could conceivably diminish to about the level it had reached in 1914 on the eve of World War I. He added that his view was based on the assumption that we would not find an immediate solution to the problem of the energy deficit that the world is experiencing due to the depletion of oil reserves.

While not reflecting a majority opinion, the group predicting a back-to-low-energy scenario envision a future of potential turmoil and disorder as more and more people compete for dwindling and irreplaceable resources. They see portentous changes resulting in a retreat from an energy-intensive culture in the Western world.

4. *Authoritarian solutions.* Although there was considerable scoffing in the mid-1970s when Robert Heilbroner spoke of a possible drift toward authoritarian controls to curb socioeconomic ills, at least some of our panelists now tend to agree.[2] While no one said so as bluntly as Heilbroner, a number of panel members stressed the need

[2]Robert Heilbroner, *An Inquiry into the Human Prospect* (New York: W. W. Norton, 1974).

for more socially responsible persons, for more exacting educational standards, and for a society that was sufficiently regulated to protect further abuses of the biosphere. A representative statement came from panelist Lynton K. Caldwell: "For the world of the West, there is the possibility that both personal freedom and social welfare policies may have reached a peak, or at least a plateau, after more than 200 years of progress."

5. *An emerging transformation?* In one way or another, a substantial minority of panelists appeared to agree to some extent with the viewpoint expressed by Alvin Toffler in *The Third Wave*, which was published shortly after our interviews were completed:

> A powerful tide is surging across much of the world today creating a new, often bizarre environment in which to work, play, marry, raise children, or retire. In this bewildering context, businessmen swim against highly erratic economic currents; politicians see their ratings bob wildly up and down; universities, hospitals, and other institutions battle desparately against inflation. Value systems splinter and crash, while the lifeboats of family, church, and state are hurled madly about.[3]

Frequently mentioned by our panelists is the need for major transformations in contemporary lifestyles, particularly with respect to greater conservation, diminished pollution, and greater equity among peoples of the world. These can come about only at the expense of standards of living in the industrially developed nations. A widely respected British thinker, Sir Geoffrey Vickers, told us that the future looked dark and uncertain, not because we lack technological skill but because of the changes created by scientific-technological developments in such areas as biology and nuclear physics. The need for social and political transformation, he felt, was especially urgent because the line between tyranny and anarchy was becoming more and more indistinct.

The explicit nature of the transformation anticipated by some panelists is not clear, but one panelist, biologist W. Jackson Davis, presented a representative "transformationalist" point of view in one of his recent publications:

> We may be witnessing no less than the grand finale of the Industrial Age, one of history's monumental cycles closing as yet another opens; and we are the privileged participants in this drama. As the

---

[3]Alvin Toffler, *The Third Wave* (New York: William Morrow and Company, Inc., 1980), p. 18.

drama unfolds, let us keep in mind that the cycles of nature and history imply continuous renewal.[4]

A composite view. It is an intriguing phenomenon in the natural sciences that, given the same data, learned persons often come to markedly different conclusions. Such disparities are even more common in the social sciences! In the view of the diverse images of tomorrow inferred from our scholars' statements, and with due regard for their impeccable credentials, it seems prudent to conclude that all of the preceding five images may in part be "true." If such a composite be accepted, then we may well expect that some aspects of tomorrow will be improved versions of today. It also seems certain that we shall continue to find scientific-technological solutions or partial "fixes" to many of our difficulties. Even the oil shortfall crisis may be eased (albeit with increased cost to consumers) as shale, residual oil deposits, and the like are exploited. Nonetheless, changes in our energy futures (involving greater use of solar panels, for instance) seem likely.

Authoritarian solutions, even in capitalist and socialist democracies, are already on the horizon in the form of "legislated behaviors," such as the 55-mile-per-hour speed limit in the U.S. Furthermore, when we consider that only about 30 of the more than 150 nations represented in the United Nations are democracies, it is clear that authoritarianism is still very much with us! Whether the transformation of the industrialized world is evolutionary or comes about as a form of mandatory social engineering, some major changes are inevitable as we strive to shift from remaking the planet for our comfort and convenience to learning how to live with the limitations its resources impose.

Without too much compromise, then, it seems that we can accept a composite of all five core positions, recognizing that part of any of the images could become reality, and move toward the future with their implications in mind.

In fairness, before coming to the end of this section, it is important to mention that some of our panelists such as Roberto Vacca and Sabino Acquaviva have warned of possible catastrophic scenarios which might lead in Vacca's words, to "a coming dark age" of hopelessness. While it is important to bear in mind that a megafamine,[5] nuclear holocausts, or other disasters are possible, there is no

[4]W. Jackson Davis, *The Seventh Year* (New York: W. W. Norton, 1979), p. 283.

[5]In the parlance of futurists, *megafamine* implies starvation for a minimum of 50 million. At present, at least one million die each year from nutritional deficits and up to 10 or 12 million suffer brain damage and physical impairment due to inadequate nutrition.

point in writing about and believing in educating for a new millennium in a context that precludes civilized survival and decent, satisfying, humane living in that millennium.

Sources of Turbulence and Likelihood of Progress

Let us consider now what sources of turbulence are likely to vex us during the next quarter century and what are the hopes for progress. The nature of the potential turbulence in tomorrow's world will be evident in the paragraphs that follow.[6] The promise of human progress is less evident. It depends on the faith that human reason will lead us to exercise wise judgment as we face the problems creating turbulence and attempt to solve them.

Scholarly threads. Despite the diverse national and academic backgrounds of the scholars interviewed, there were a number of similarities that ran through their comments on the world of the future producing an "intradisciplinary thread phenomenon."[7] For example, *natural* scientists often drew on the substantive content of the *social* sciences or addressed themselves to the problems in the social sciences, and vice versa. So complex have the world's problems become that biologists, for instance, often see their research in a societal context. Conversely, a political scientist is likely to be engaged in studying the implications of physical resource depletion for the human community.

Values in collision. The study of the viewpoints from our panel of scholars with respect to both turbulence and progress in the Eighties and Nineties is made difficult by the fact that the panelists' concepts in the physical sciences, and particularly in the social sciences, are likely to vary from one country to another. Certain political and philosophical premises tend to be "locked in" with fields such as economics or political science. For example, the phrases "human rights" or "democratization" do not convey the same meanings in Washington or Moscow, Madrid or Singapore, Peking or London. In the West, rights are likely to be associated with individual welfare. In a communist country individual rights are subordinate to the welfare of the state. From a Russian's point of view, to "democratize education"

---

[6]Panelist Michael Marien reviewed 1,603 abstracts which subsequently appeared in *Future Survey 1979*. His eight major areas of concern as mirrored in the literature coincided with the sources of turbulence reviewed here with respect to values, nuclear weapons, pollution-energy-resource depletion, economic problems, and electronic technologies. See Marien's summary in *The Futurist* (June 1980), pp. 3-9.

[7]The thread phenomenon is discussed in more detail in chapter 3.

means to provide *equal access*, which is quite different from John Dewey's ideas about democracy in education.

Nowhere was this conflict in values more evident that at Unesco in Paris where we conducted some of the interviews for this study. In this polycultural setting one panelist stated, "Unesco, conceived as a place to draw us together for worthy purposes, instead has begun to resemble an arena in which to trade abuse while maneuvering to serve national purposes."

Lester R. Brown commented some years ago that we were in grave danger of being betrayed by values, "inherited largely from the past," that are now inconsistent with human survival. Brown, president of Worldwatch, is both a natural and a social scientist and was one of the early proponents of the "green revolution" using improved grain strains to increase crop yields. In *World Without Borders* he writes, "Not only are many of man's institutions incapable of resolving the problem he now faces, but his values, inherited from the past, are inconsistent with his survival. Values which are widely held . . . are becoming threats to our future well-being. Man must evolve a new social ethic. . . ."[8]

The sources of possible turbulence presented below are but a few of the many changes nations must cope with in coming years if the next century is to see us attain a more decent and humane world.

Competing values and ideologies. Foremost among our contemporary problems is the struggle between the proponents of *autonomy* and the proponents of *organic interdependence*. The former are dedicated to unrestricted growth and to the continued improvement of the material quality of life, while the latter advocate conservation and the frugal use of planetary resources. The autonomists are guided by a 19th century "frontier ethic," a time when we had seemingly boundless land, untrammeled and open to exploitation. No band of frontiersmen, no wagon train of settlers, could do widespread damage to the vastness about them as they trickled beyond the Mississippi River to breach the Rocky Mountain barrier and eventually to reach to Pacific coast.

The idea of a nation with inexhaustible resources was well established in the U.S. early in the 20th century. Then the frontiers began to close down. After World War II, the European colonial powers, who controlled 85% of the earth's resources and influenced the lives of perhaps 70% of the world population, began gradually to lose the sources of cheap energy and inexpensive raw materials provided by their colonies. By the 1950s a few prescient thinkers such as panelist Sir

[8]See Lester R. Brown, *World Without Borders* (New York: Random House, 1972).

Geoffrey Vickers began to describe the concept of organic interdependence and to advocate "a spaceship ethic" to replace the frontier ethic.[9]

The spaceship ethic conceives our planet as a closed ecosystem, which requires a balance between humankind and nature. Along with the idea of ecological balance is the concept of equitable sharing among its human passengers. At present, if spaceship earth had but five passengers, *one* passenger (the industrialized world) would have 80% of its life support resources. The other *four* passengers (the less developed nations) would have but 5% each.[10]

As we move into the 1980s, the frontier versus the spaceship ethic promises to remain a source of conflict. The subsequent, ineluctable tension will create much turbulence. At the same time, the growing international recognition of the spaceship ethic has created a worldwide dialogue as to how to avoid ecological catastrophies and incinerating the planet with violence of modern weaponry.

Democratic institutions under stress. The machinery of democracy designed by the Founding Fathers at the Constitutional Convention in Philadelphia during the 1780s was an extraordinary amalgam of wisdom and foresight. Written on the threshold of a new industrialized age, the Constitution has proved remarkably viable in the face of social, technological, and economic changes that could not possibly have been anticipated by its designers.

Today, however, with national and international events occurring more and more rapidly and with the media overwhelming us with images, the machinery of democratic governments is under stress and shows signs of increasing strain. The turbulence stemming from confused and erroneous governmental decision making were manifest in the 1960s and became even more conspicuous in the 1970s.

Since 1900 Americans have improved working conditions in factories, ended exploitive child labor, enfranchised women, and advanced human rights. Such initiatives are to be prized. At the same time, as a number of panelists pointed out, how are the processes of democracy to be protected in the 1980s from increasing self-serving demands which seem likely to imperil the idea of representative government?

---

[9]See Sir Geoffrey Vickers' Wilde Memorial Lecture, "Some Ideas of Progress" (1954), and his "Ecology, Planning, and the American Dream" (1963) in Leonard J. Duhl, ed., *The Urban Condition*. His two BBC lectures on "The End of Free Fall" also are examples of his insights into resource depletion and threats to the biosphere, which were then little recognized. The lectures are reprinted in his *Value Systems and Social Process* (Harmondsworth, Middlesex, England: Penguin Books, Ltd., 1970).

[10]The writer is indebted to Father Theodore M. Hesburgh, President, the University of Notre Dame, who originally suggested the five passenger spaceship illustration.

Demands, expectations, and pressures for what Daniel Bell has called "entitlements" are growing as various interest groups maneuver for power. If candidates for elective office can rely on 40% of the electorate for support, and can write off another 40% as implacable opponents, they then must appeal to the 20% minority swing vote to win a majority at the polls. In this small group are the innumerable single issue voters who pressure candidates to support their special interests in exchange for their support. Over the years this pressure for privilege has come from religious, ethnic, labor, business, and industry lobbies.

In addition to the threat of pressure groups, a second threat to democratic institutions, according to some panelists, is the diminished capacity of the government to make prompt, sound decisions. Repeatedly, government advisors failed to advise officials, made faulty predictions that have damaged the standard of living, harmed the U.S. image overseas, diminished the strength of our democracy, and resulted in such recent national embarrassments as those associated with Vietnam, Cuba, and Iran. The proliferation of bureaucracies to deal with problems has merely diffused the problem without solving it. Furthermore, the use of computers by advisory agencies sometimes does no more than insure that errors can be made more quickly! Our institutional lag presumably needs to be remedied in every echelon and at all levels if growing mistrust of governing officials is to be alleviated.

Population and hunger. Population pressures promise to become increasingly dangerous. Some 12,000 years ago the world population numbered about 12 million, roughly the population of Greater London today. The first billion mark was not reached until some time shortly after 1860.

Improved medical care, sanitation, and the development of various wonder drugs have helped to extend the life span dramatically in recent years. By 1975 the population exceeded four billion. At present, according to Garrett Hardin, there is a net increase of approximately 220,000 mouths to be fed each day—the equivalent of a Chicago added every fortnight. It is likely that the global population will increase to between six and seven billion by early in the 21st century. While there are some encouraging signs that birthrates are coming down, this is not the case in many less developed countries. An increase of over two billion inhabitants in a few decades will not only test the earth's carrying capacity, it will have a profound impact on sociopolitical decision making.

Since much of the population increase over the next 20 years is likely to be in the countries with the least natural resources (Bangladesh, India, Indonesia, for example), there exists the sorry prospect of more and more children with frail bodies and hunger-damaged minds. By the mid-Seventies the World Development Corporation estimated that as many as one million humans were dying annually from starvation, often in their first year of life; and each year as many as 10 million suffer from irreparable mental and physical damage due to malnutrition. Pressure for a larger share of the world's food supply has increased in the have-less countries and has placed a growing moral burden on more fortunate countries.

The rich and the poor. At present, the population of the less developed nations includes over three billion or in excess of 75% of the total world population. These nations are extremely poor. In the mid-1970s the U.S. Agency for International Development reported to Congress the following "development gap" information:[11]

Indicator	Developing Countries	Developed Countries	United States
1. Per Capita GNP	$230	$3,085	$4,756
2. Population (millions)	1,850	664	207
3. Literacy	40%	97%	98%
4. Life Expectancy	52 years	71 years	70 years
5. Annual per capita power consumption	220 kwh	5140 kwh	8100 kwh

More vivid than the figures above is the picture drawn by Robert L. Heilbroner.[12] He states that for a typical family living on from $70 to $200 per capita, there would be no more than a few blankets, a couple of pieces of furniture, and one garment for each person plus one pair of shoes for the head of the household. Their home, no larger than a toolshed, would have no water and no electricity, no books or magazines (of what use would they be to the illiterate?), and no access to medical care save for a local midwife. The family's cash hoard would come to no more than five dollars, and the annual cash crop income from the three tenant acres would be shared with the local money lender and their landlord. Because of these conditions, as one scholar-panelist saw it, there is growing pressure not merely for a *new deal*, but for a new *order.*[13]

[11]*The U.S. and The Developing World*, abridged (Washington, D.C.: Overseas Development Council, 1973), p. 123.

[12]Adapted from his *The Great Ascent.*

[13]Geoffrey Barraclough, "The World Economic Struggle," *New York Review of Books*, August 1975, pp. 23-30.

Barbara Ward provided a vivid analogy when she pointed out that internationally there is bitter resentment on the part of the Third World similar to the sullen and rebellious attitudes found among peasants in Czarist Russia or in France at the time of their respective revolutions.[14] The disparity between the haves and have-nots also helps to explain the illconcealed lack of sympathy in certain Third World countries when the U.S. is discomfited, for example, in dealing with a Fidel Castro in Cuba or an Ayatollah Khomeini in Iran. Particularly, in the UN the have-less nations, who make up the majority of the membership, have expressed their resentment and feel they are entitled to make claims on the wealth of the have-more nations, particularly the U.S. Their assumption is that, since in the post-imperalist industrialized world there is a vast fund of unethically accumulated wealth to be shared, some forms of reparations are due.

Ironically, the U.S. is one among a few nations that endorses a share-the-wealth global social policy. The U.S. was the first nation in history to initiate vast income transfers to other nations through such agencies as the Marshall Plan, after World War II; Point Four, during President Truman's administration; the Act for International Development (AID), and the International Cooperation Administration (ICA). Beginning with a commitment of two percent of America's Gross National Product (GNP) after World War II, the total income transfer as of 1980 runs to the tens of billions of dollars. Yet by the mid-Seventies, developed countries, including the U.S., found themselves accused of being responsible for the starvation of little children because of their excessive consumption of foodstuffs and other material goods.

The disorderliness of the present decade in the UN is further exacerbated by the substantial representation of small countries, of which some 120-odd are, to a certain extent, controlled, authoritarian societies. In the General Assembly members such as Singapore, with a third or a quarter of the population of a city such as Tokyo, New York, or Mexico City, has the same voice and vote as the largest nation. Since the political independence of the Third World nations did not necessarily bring them economic independence, we can expect the drive for greater, more equitable sharing of the world's goods will remain a source of transnational tension during the 1980s.

Danger of sophisticated weapons and nuclear accidents. Controversies over nuclear policy and the sale of sophisticated weapons promise to increase during the 1980s. As the world's leading arms ex-

---

[14]Barbara Ward, *Progress for a Small Planet* (New York: W. W. Norton, 1979), p. 170.

porter, the U.S. is a prime target for those who are alarmed over how, and on whom, the lethal weapons might be used.[15]

The following concerns seem certain to create widespread anxiety:

• Yet to be determined damage to the biosphere caused by the deadly radiation released when nuclear weapons are detonated;

• Dangers in nuclear plants inadequately designed or poorly built;

• The prospect of suitcase-size nuclear bombs in the hands of terrorists;

• The plutonium by-product from nuclear plants both as an ingredient in nuclear bombs and as a deadly carcinogenic threat;

• Disposal of nuclear reactor waste which remains lethal for untold generations;

• Nuclear proponents who contend that the growing demand for power in a heavily populated world leaves no choice but to exploit the atom in order to meet their energy needs.

Scholars suggest that if we are to resolve nuclear and weaponry dilemmas, we must endeavor to see that American nuclear policy becomes the precursor of positive arms restraint, that we carefully sift information pertaining to nuclear power, and that we make every effort to increase quickly the knowledge of the safe handling of toxic wastes.

Pollution and resource depletion. The twin spectres of pollution and continued dwindling of resources seem certain to haunt humans during the next 25 years, according to the panel of international scholars. The turmoil will come from our apparent inability to reconcile extravagant lifestyles with their drain on the biosphere.

Barry Commoner, one of the scholars in biology invited to serve on our panel wrote about the problem back in the 1960s:

> The environment is a complex, subtly balanced system, and it is this integrated whole which receives the impact of all the separate insults inflicted by pollutants. Never before in the history of this planet has its thin life-supporting surface been subjected to such diverse, novel, and potent agents. I believe that the cumulative effects of these pollutants, their interactions and amplification, can be fatal to the complex fabric of the biosphere. And because man is, after all, dependent on part of this system, I believe that continued pollution of the earth, if unchecked, will eventually destroy the fitness of this planet as a place for human life.[16]

---

[15] As of 1980, the Soviet Union is the number two exporter; France is number three.

[16] Because of his participation in the 1980 presidential campaign, Commoner was unable to schedule an interview with our project staff. Barry Commoner, *Science and Survival*, in *Saturday Review*, 20 September 1969, p. 56.

With such explicit warnings, and they were frequent in our interviews, when will we mobilize against environmental threats? As Sir Geoffrey Vickers put it, we ventilate mines and irrigate deserts "on purpose" and pollute rivers and poison the atmosphere "by accident."[17] As pressure increases to prevent such "accidents" in the closing years of the century, it is bound to create turmoil.

Inflation, debt, and unemployment. The interlinked elements of inflation, mounting debt, and unemployment have become increasingly dangerous, worldwide phenomena. Coping with them will test our capacity for economic innovation as we move into the uneasy Eighties. These elements may even prove to be symptomatic of the inability of world economic systems to accommodate themselves to declining per capita productivity. Furthermore, as pointed out in chapter 1, these three elements tend to lower the standard of living of the have-less groups—those with limited economic or political clout.

The extent of the inflationary trends is reflected in 1980 data from the U.S. Departments of Labor and Commerce and the International Monetary Fund. In one recent 12-month period representative increases in consumer prices were:[18]

Argentina	150.1%	France	11.8%
Brazil	76.0%	Canada	9.5%
Italy	20.4%	Japan	5.7%
Britain	18.4%	Switzerland	5.1%
U.S.	14.1%	West Germany	4.6%

The profoundly troubling issue of inflation during the present decade was identified by a number of our panelists. Their conclusion is that there is no instant solution for skyrocketing inflation. A basic reason may prove to be that more and more persons—at least two billion more by 2006—are now and will continue to be competing for the same diminishing raw materials, living space, and for food for survival.

Attempting to cope with inflation by using the strategy of indexing, an income transfer system which automatically boosts wages, welfare benefits, and pensions, has become extremely expensive for many governments. As of mid-1980, approximately 65 million Americans as well as millions of Europeans had some form of "index insurance" against inflation. Social Security payments (increased by

---

[17]In his 1954 essay, "Some Ideas of Progress."

[18]*U.S. News and World Report*, 7 April 1980, p. 32.

14.3% in July of 1980) led the list with 35,300,000 recipients.[19] The rationale for the indexing is both obvious and appealing—humane treatment of the aged, the sick, and the poor. Millions of men and women in Europe also have salaries and pensions which increase automatically because they are geared to the inflation rate.[20]

Since it would be politically difficult to modify government obligations such as social security, the future is likely to be a stormy one:

- as taxpayer resistance grows;
- as the young resent increasingly large federal withholding in paychecks to pay for social security costs for the elderly;
- as the governments seek ways of reconciling indexing and inflation—including taxing social security payments;
- as defense spending and other major budget items compete for federal funds; and
- as persons without automatically increasing incomes express resentment toward indexing or demand regular pay boosts as inflation continues.

Mounting debt also gravely concerns economists. Not only has increasing governmental debt become chronic but personal debt in the U.S. during the last ten years has skyrocketed. In 1970, private debt (e.g., mortgages, auto loans, credit card payments) totaled less than $500 billion. By 1978 it came to $1 trillion, $165 billion! By 1980, due to government credit controls, the rate of increase had slowed but the huge burden nonetheless kept growing. As Edward Cornish phrased it, "In the U.S. today most households probably are both illiquid and in debt; they have little money available in cash or in the bank, and they owe thousands of dollars on past purchases."[21]

A third source of turmoil is global unemployment. Estimates vary, but between 800 and 900 million persons probably were out of work or underemployed at the outset of the Eighties. There is potential "social dynamite" here in the form of discontent and rebellion—dynamite in need of rapid defusing. But ways of coping will not be

---

[19]Other persons with indexed cost of living benefits included recipients of supplemental security, 4,188,000; retired federal civilian employees, 1,712,000; retired military personnel, 1,308,000; railroad retirees, 1,006,000; disabled coal miners, 416,000; war veterans with pensions, 2,167,000; postal workers, 656,000; union members with escalator clauses, 2,200,000; state and local government workers and retirees, 1,450,000; food stamp recipients, 20,200,000. Reported in *U.S. News and World Report*, 9 June 1980, p. 50.

[20]It was calculated in London during 1980 that the pension-indexed retired head of Scotland Yard, if he remained alive until 1999, would receive nearly $500,000 per year at current British inflation rates!

[21]Edward Cornish, "The Great Depression of the 1980s: Could It Really Happen?" *The Futurist*, October 1979, p. 366.

easy, since they seem invariably to threaten large segments of the population.

Rising aspirations turning to rising frustrations. Until the mid-1960s a mood of general optimism pervaded the U.S. The dollar was strong, the technological triumph of moon landings created and sustained a wave of national pride, and there was confidence that the spread of Communism could be contained. Furthermore the standard of living in America kept rising each year. As recently as the mid-Seventies a survey in Kansas City and Boston indicated that "average" Americans still were confident that they could attain the good life, described by those surveyed as an income of about $25,000 a year, a four-bedroom home in the suburbs, two automobiles, and an annual three-week vacation.[22]

As the 1970s wore on, this materialistic dream began to fade. Purchasing power decreased, established institutions (government, labor unions, the corporate community, churches, schools, and so on) became objects of mistrust, and America's world image was diminished by a series of disturbing national and international developments including the humiliating war in Vietnam, an unprecedented presidential resignation, and the taking of 52 hostages with the seizure of our embassy in Iran.

The realization that the "revolution of rising human expectations" might not materialize brought with it a profound sense of frustration. The citizens of have-more nations saw their hope of continuing upward mobility first threatened and then replaced by fear of possible socioeconomic losses. The inhabitants of have-less countries were alarmed at the prospect of remaining forever poor, of never having a larger slice of the international economic pie.

As this is written, the rising level of global frustration may well become one of the major dangers involving both domestic tranquility and international cooperation.

The electronic assault on human reason. Virtually all those born since 1950 have been exposed throughout their lives to the electronic medium, television. The barrage of images provides some knowledge (or at least information) but, as a number of scholars see it, television also makes an assult on reason and on emotional stability, as it transmits the wrenching world changes that have occurred since 1950.

Television is a particularly powerful and mind-shaping force in the U.S. due to the sheer magnitude of its programming. It is even

---

[22]Directed by Richard Coleman, Senior Research Associate, the Joint Center for Urban Studies of M.I.T. and Harvard University; cited by *Time*, 8 February 1976, p. 107.

more powerful in portraying the U.S. image to the Third World. Third World viewers see lifestyles in the U.S. depicted in a manner that incites envy, for such lifestyles are beyond the reach of the Nigerian in Enugu or the Pakistani in Lahore. Moreover, Third World citizens frequently are unable to differentiate between the realities of U.S. culture and the follies transmitted by television. The effect of this discrepancy is tension and turbulence. Unfortunately, no *cordon sanitaire* can be established to protect the real image of the American citizen from the degenerate ones that often entertain her citizens on television. Another source of emotional strain occurs when the poor in the U.S. see portrayed on the television screen a standard of living that seems futile for them to attempt to reach.

Another concern expressed by some scholars is that not only do people throughout the world see America reflected in a distorting mirror, but we are now continually exposed to global coverage of events—often disasters—which require us to worry about everyone and everything everywhere. The sense of uneasiness or even incipient panic that may result is not the best of bases for reasoned behavior. Also, as panelist Lawrence Cremin pointed out, there is a danger of inadvertent thought control because of the selective nature of items featured in newscasts, which must be squeezed into the narrow grooves of time available in daily schedules. After hearing disturbing news, the programs tend to end with the so-called wrap-up, which summarizes what has been seen, what it means, and even what might be expected tomorrow.[23] "That's the way it is," does not necessarily describe the real world to all viewers at all times!

One more manifestation of the electronic incursion is the viewing habits of children (under five years of age) and of youth, who are often exposed to TV for as long as eight hours a day. The tube becomes the baby-sitter, or it entertains the baby-sitters themselves, or it absorbs parents when they return home, thus extending the young child's viewing time. Furthermore, children's programs, notably on Saturday morning, tend to feature cartoons of dubious psychological value, often lacking in educational merit. They are likely to show some sort of super hero or heroine miraculously solving problems, all of which suggest that humanity's misadventures and disasters can only be solved through the efforts of a "great leader," usually authoritarian.[24]

---

[23]For a longer inquiry into selective newscasting, see Ward Just, "Newspaper Days: Politics—We Are the Hostages," *The Atlantic*, April 1980, pp. 99-101.

[24]For the opinion of a learned panel, see "Children's Television: What Are the Best—and Worst—Shows?" *TV Guide*, 9 August 1980, pp. 2-6.

Inane television commercials show young and old alike responding mindlessly to carbonated beverages, a new laundry soap, or decaffeinated coffee in a manner at best naive and at worst downright idiotic. The display of adults' childish behavior over toilet paper or a brand of instant coffee does little to enhance young viewers' respect for their elders, even though youngsters are surprisingly sophisticated about advertising hokum.

By the time our youth graduate from high school they have spent more time televiewing (16,000 hours) than in the classroom (12,000 hours). Watching television not only takes away time from home study, it cuts down on socializing, exercise, and time for learning experiences that ultimately influence "intelligence." Television was identified as one of the causes of the decline in test scores by former Secretary of Labor Willard Wirtz and a panel established by the College Entrance Examination board.[25]

A final point—TV confuses our reason, our time sense, and our feeling for "real world" geography by jumbling so many impressions into too few minutes. In a half hour viewers can choose between a World War II movie, a show spectacular, an interview with a celebrity, or a situation comedy—all periodically interrupted by commercials. During the same period a tornado watch warning may glide silently across the screen, or a "news break" may bring word of a flare-up in yet another corner of the globe. Small wonder our nervous system circuits become overloaded!

As a source of malaise, as a reminder of the horrors to which people in many parts of the world are subjected, and by its subtle pervasiveness, television has become recognized by some scholars as a potent threat to rational, studied decisions. As one panelist said, "If we ever are forced to choose up sides for the apocalypse, you can be sure that television will be shaping our decisions!"

The Speed of Change: The Crisis of Crises

The 10 examples of forces, factors, and developments contributing to present-day turbulence also carry a promise of progress for the planet as people learn how to deal with them. Although not always immediately apparent, progress depends on the efforts human beings must make by instituting self-preserving (as distinct from self-serving) reforms in order to counter or resolve this turmoil.

What needs to be accomplished will require patience. Results may

---

[25]See "The Academic Score Decline: Are Facts the Enemy of Truth?" *Phi Delta Kappan*, October 1977, pp. 85-86. (An interview with W. Willard Wirtz.)

seem infinitely slow; people everywhere will need to remember that while they can see only the second hand move, the hour hand is also moving! The spirit of the era dare not become tired of too much change, because so many profound and positive changes are in order.

The crisis of crises.[26] The mayor in a large city can usually cope with emergencies such as a heavy snowfall, strikes by police or firemen, or a derailed train with chemical-filled tank cars. But if the train derails in a massive snowfall at the same time that police and firemen are on strike, a full-blown crisis is created.

For the past two decades the world has been building up to its present crisis of crises stage. To paraphrase Murphy's Law, "What *could* go wrong *did* go wrong!" One of our challenges today is to make tomorrow work by repealing Murphy's Law and initiating the changes that are called for now and in the years that lie ahead.

One insight which rapid change requires is that we recognize existent interdependence of human beings and world resources. The increasing use of the automobile in an energy-short world provides a good illustration of this interdependence.

Automobiles as illustrative of technological traps. In the minds of many people the automobile has replaced the dog as man's best friend. Nothing could be further from the truth! Actually, automobiles have created *microcrises* which (as the situation becomes better understood) may provide guidelines for dealing with *macrocrises.*

Between 1960 and 1978 the world's car fleet more than tripled.[27] In these 18 years the number of vehicles leaped from 98 to 302 million! Since the U.S. is so heavily dependent on the automobile, the automotive crisis in the Eighties and Nineties is a topic close to home. About 85% of the world's cars are licensed in the U.S., Canada, Britain, Germany and France; hence these countries are certain to be among those most profoundly affected.

Here are some of the multiple problems surrounding the future of the auto:

> The demand for cars is increasing rapidly. In Japan alone since 1960, ownership has increased from one million to over 34 million! However, with petroleum in increasingly short supply, with vast price increases for oil, with growing pollution problems, along with enormous traffic problems, it seems impossible to envision 600 million cars by 1999. Yet this is where a *linear* projection leads us when

---

[26]The term "crisis of crises" was used originally by one of our panelists, biophysicist John Platt.

[27]The data cited are taken from "Worldwatch Paper 32," *The Future of the Automobile in an Oil-Short World* (Washington, D.C.: Worldwatch Institute, 1979).

current trends are extrapolated. Where, then, do we turn for a solution?

> Because of the way in which housing construction has gone in the U.S., with great diffusion of population to suburbs and rural areas, many persons are too removed from services to get along without personal auto transport. Where do we go from here?
>
> On a global basis, 30 million people directly or indirectly depend on the truck or automobile business. In the U.S., 22% of the work force is in the automotive sector! How shall we avoid or at least diminish the economic consequences which are intimately involved in a switch to mass transportation?

These factors: increasing demand for cars and decreasing oil reserves; current dependence on auto transportation in many parts of the globe; and the economic dependence of tens of millions of people on auto-related jobs serve to illustrate a technological trap. Perhaps for the foreseeable future we could manage to deal effectively with any one of the factors, but in combination they pose an enormous puzzle to be solved.

One of our panelists, Geoffrey Vickers, foresaw with extraordinary clarity the dilemmas of cause and effect:

> Men may release into the milieu a virus which destroys rabbits, and may develop a fertilizer industry which displaces sheep. No longer destroyed by sheep and rabbits, the coarse growth may displace the finer herbage. Woods may rise to overshadow their own seedbed so densely that only fungus will grow there. The self-destroyed wood may fail to let in the light and destroy the fungus....
>
> [Analogous] is the process whereby men build cities and cities attract men; cities breed plagues and plagues limit the size of cities; men curb plagues and cities expand into vast and formless aggregates, from which men try to escape. The automobile brings a means of escape for a few; the many follow and choke the roads. The roads multiply and let the traffic through; the roads and traffic carry with them the megalopolis from which they are flying.[28]

Transition or Transformation?

Futurists during the late Seventies engaged in wide speculation as to whether or not the industrial era, as it presently is constituted, can survive. As noted in chapter 1, a growing literature questions whether

---

[28]Geoffrey Vickers, "Ecology, Planning and the American Dream," in *The Urban Condition; People and Policy in the Metropolis*, ed. Leonard F. Duhl with John Powell (New York: Basic Books, 1963).

the industrialized world can go through a *transitional* period leading to a viable future, or whether a profound *transformation* lies ahead.[29]

A major question is *shall* and *can* we strive for reforms within the present system, or does the chaos of the present argue for a massive reassessment and possible realignment of our lifestyles? Will we, with the help of microelectronics and robotics, usher in a new era comparable in impact to the Renaissance of the 14th, 15th, and 16th centuries during which changes in art and architecture, literature, and learning, heralded the emergence of modern times from the chrysalis of medievalism? Will this, then, be the new millennium?

The human riddle. Given the necessary insight, will U.S. youth and adults alike have the courage to come to terms with nature and with their psychological, physical, and sociological environment as well as with their world peer groups?[30] Or will they elect to retain a sybaritic culture that will, as long as possible, be nonthreatening and amusing to its creatures—a peurile soap opera culture?

Here we find ourselves recycled to the educational challenge of chapter 1: how to cope and improve our present levels of thinking and acting, rooted as they are in a world in which traditional ways of thinking and acting often are neither adequate nor relevant.[31]

Curriculum Content and the Future

The present turbulence, which seems certain to continue well into the future, has distinct implications for curriculum content. This is true regardless of the way in which "curriculum" is defined. The questions are: How does one *educate* for effective living in an era of turmoil? How do we help learners of all ages grasp survival concepts, understand how to use them wisely, and work with others in creating a more humane, less threatening world society?

Action learning and service experiences. At least since the 1930s educators have advocated learning experiences that extend beyond the school walls.[32] Today's speed of change and the serious nature of

---

[29]See Appendix D for studies reported by Lester R. Brown, W. Jackson Davis, Marilyn Ferguson, Willis Harman, James Robertson, Alvin Toffler, and Barbara Ward with information on possible societal transitions.

[30]Stuart Chase, over thirty years ago, also identified these as the two "Great Questions" in *The Proper Study of Mankind* (New York: Harper and Brothers, 1948), p. 305.

[31]For a stimulating discussion of this point, several panelists mentioned and recommended a Club of Rome report by J. W. Botkin, Mahdi Elmandjra, and Mircea Malitza, *No Limits to Learning: Bridging the Human Gap* (Oxford: Pergamon Press, 1979), p. 118 ff.

[32]For a detailed statement of the development of "learning beyond school walls" see Appendix A.

global problems, which lead to turbulence and to wide-scale disorder, make such extended learning more important than ever.

Traditional education with its red tape and regulations, its passivity and "right" answers, is the old way of doing things. The demands of the present and of the future clearly call for new ways of doing things. Active, dynamic experiences, sponsored by the school but going beyond its confines, help to satisfy this need. Service learning involving socially useful work supplies an added ingredient—significant participation. Together they will help students to cope wisely and successfully with new developments and to participate willingly and well in the interminable task of envisioning and inventing the future.

3

Basic Concepts: The Natural Sciences

[Humans] have perhaps ten years left in which to subordinate their ancient quarrels and launch a global partnership to curb the arms race, to improve the human environment, to defuse the population explosion and to supply the required momentum to development efforts.

—U Thant

In the previous chapter, we stitched together a verbal tapestry that anticipates tomorrow and that also implies the need for an "anticipatory curriculum" in a new era. We can now attempt to weave together the concepts suggested by our panel of scholars in the natural and social sciences and endeavor to determine what they imply for curriculum content.

With the decline in natural resources, the problems of a deteriorating environment, and increased international tensions, certain concepts basic to effective living in the years ahead assume added significance. As we interpreted the testimony from our interviews and from written response from our panelists, we recognized how complicated the task of reporting their diverse viewpoints and drawing inferences would be.

As chapter 2 indicated, five conflicting views of the future were directly or indirectly expressed by our panelists. These views suggested the problem of reconciling certain divergent views preserved in our data. An example of such conflicting opinion in the same field of inquiry is illustrated by the diametrically opposed views of Harrell R. Rogers and Morton Paglin on the issue of poverty in the U.S. In his *Poverty Amid Plenty*, Rogers contends that the U.S. government underestimates the breadth and depth of poverty.[1] Paglin, on the

[1]Harrell R. Rogers, Jr., *Poverty Amid Plenty: A Political and Economic Analysis* (Reading, Maine: Addison-Wesley Press, 1979).

other hand, and with access to the same sources, insists that official surveys actually overestimate the extent of the problem.[2] Another example is the controversy surrounding interpretations of the 1980 U.S. Census data which can be construed in various ways for personal or for political advantage.

Nevertheless, nearly all scholars interviewed were in consensus regarding such omnipresent problems as the energy deficit and the pollution of our environment. Also, they tended to agree on the concepts that are important for young people to learn. But they disagreed on the ways certain contemporary problems should be resolved. For example, on the issue of "limits to growth," the panelists, while recognizing the need to reduce consumption, differed as to how we should impose limitations to growth.

Assumptions about a "surprise-free" future. Many of the concepts inventoried in chapters 3 and 4 are based on the assumption that a "surprise-free" future lies ahead of us, not disrupted by nuclear accidents such as occurred in 1945 when a twenty-kiloton nuclear bomb was dropped on Hiroshima. For example, it was taken for granted by most panelists that there was no short-term (5-6 year) solution to the energy shortage and probably no long-term (20-25 year) prospect of finding an equally efficient, safe, substitute for petroleum as an energy source for industrial societies. However, a breakthrough could be made—a surprise breakthrough that would strengthen industrial societies. For instance, ways might be found to eliminate some of the dangers inherent in nuclear plants.

The future, when it becomes the present, is full of such surprises, some ugly, some benign. Twenty years ago, who would have forecast the dramatic changes and troubling developments that made ugly headlines: blocks of Washington, D.C. and Watts district of Los Angeles afire as a result of rioting; the assassination of a President, his brother, and a distinguished black leader; widespread unrest, bombings, and students gunned down on the college campus; a tragic war and its aftermath in Southeast Asia; or the global impact of an OPEC oil embargo on world economies? More promising surprises have been the invention of new life forms, DNA splicing; hybridization in plants to increase yields; development of the silicon chip and improved computer technology, and new means of population control.

While we can accept expert opinion and prognosis, we also must remain sufficiently fluid in thinking about and planning for the future in order to accommodate ourselves to the unexpected or the un-

---

[2]Morton Paglin, "Poverty in the United States: A Reevaluation," *Policy Review*, Spring 1979, pp. 7-24.

predictable. Furthermore, our findings should be viewed with some caution since no amount of opinion, however carefully developed, can create a *fact*. Expertise, especially when pooled, merely increases the likelihood of the *opinion* being a valid one.

Transdisciplinary linkages—the "threads phenomenon." As the writer has noted elsewhere in a report on preliminary findings of this project:

> The increased use of such terms as microbiology or biophysics, as well as the appointment of professors of geography *and* history or molecular biology *and* zoology or psychology *and* neural science, suggest the increasing breadth of knowledge which contemporary scholars are expected to acquire.[3]

These cross-disciplinary trends seem both necessary and desirable, but they often make it difficult to sort out or to cluster concepts for purposes of presentation. In the natural and social sciences the "threads of knowledge" phenomenon has created, for some years now, a seamless web as a result of scholarly inquiry. This phenomenon of "seamlessness" in knowledge suggests that in the realms where the panelists work, you cannot pursue a single thing, because everything is influenced by the entire system. Thus, it is necessary to use a statement of overarching concepts in order to present certain ideas that were obtained from our panelists in the natural sciences and that in some instances were voiced by persons in the social sciences as well.

Overarching Concepts

The doctrine of limits; the need to conserve. No single concept was mentioned so often and elaborated so thoroughly as the idea of the potentially dangerous overload humans have imposed on the earth's carrying capacity. Since the publication of *The Limits to Growth* in 1972, few topics have generated stronger feelings both among scientists and among those in the corporate world.[4] Representative statements on this concept from our panel of scholars follow:

> It is important for everybody to understand, at as early an age as possible, that the earth places limitations on us. There are physical

---

[3]Harold Shane, "Probable Developments in the Social Sciences and Their Consequences for Educational Content" (Paper prepared for the Unesco Symposium: "The Evolution of Educational Content with Particular Emphasis on General Education," Paris, July, 1980).

[4]In 1976 in a conversation with the writer, David Rockefeller, president of the Chase Manhattan Bank, summarized the opinion of many corporate executives when he said ". . . people who would limit growth fail to take into account that to diminish poverty—to improve the life of billions of people living at a bare subsistence level—we *have* to have continued growth."

> limits to such numbers as the amount of oil that can be obtained from the earth and the number of people that can be placed on it. Scientific research has given us techniques to live at increasingly better levels within those limits. A sizable portion of the population, however, seems to feel that we can manipulate our way to wealth merely by political or economic tinkering. The sooner we understand physical realities, the better off we all will be.
>
> —*John J. W. Rogers*

> Students should . . . understand that man has become a powerful geological agent capable of changing rates of erosion, affecting climate, and altering the natural fluxes of energy. Some of the changes are occurring as part of what amounts to uncontrolled experiments that will influence all of us.
>
> —*Brian J. Skinner*

> The supply-demand relationship falters in the case of nonrenewable resources, as physical circumstances, rather than economic laws govern their availability.
>
> —*John B. Patton*

> Students should know that human life is wholly dependent on the earth and its resources of water, energy, minerals, soils, land, plant and animal life, and the natural environment. All of these resources are finite. They can be exhausted or despoiled by careless use. Developed, used, and reused wisely, however, they can be extended to support human life far into the future, particularly if population growth can be reduced.
>
> —*Vincent E. McKelvey*

> Students should be aware that the impermanence of the energy resource base on which our civilization is built is our present problem. Resource production is on a bell-shaped curve which rises to a peak, and after reaching the peak declines in a more or less symmetrical way.
>
> –*W. Jackson Davis*

The points made by panelists such as the five cited above varied in detail, but the central message was clear. Unless major steps are taken to conserve, to recycle, and to reduce consumption, the world, particularly the energy-dependent industrialized nations, will be plagued for years to come by the limits imposed by finite resources, by enormous population increases, and by consequent decline in global material standards of living. As noted earlier, British physicist Sir Nevill Mott, a Nobel Prize winner, speculated that by the year 2000 the per capita energy available might be no more than that which was available in 1914, unless some breakthrough occurs in the quest for an alternative to fossil fuels as a source of energy.

The doctrine of limits also raised the prospect that there would be some contraction of wealth and, quite possibly, a return to simpler lifestyles. A psychobiologist among our panelists put it this way:

> I see a contraction of material wealth which may be the fountainhead of simplicity. I think we will move forward, not backward, into a simpler life. We are going to face the future without energy, but with a population that has been generated by energy. If we don't change our values, then the depletion of energy and resources will do it for us.
>
> —*W. Jackson Davis*

Interdependence. A second major, overarching concept that youth and adults need to grasp is the increasing interdependence that exists among nations and among people everywhere. Several facets of interdependence appeared in our interviews with scientists, particularly the concept of ecological holism. As a zoologist saw it:

> In ecology, the concept of interdependence of all life and the mechanisms through which that interdependence is expressed are central themes. The flow of energy and the cycling of the biologically important forms of matter tie all living things together, and the processes of predation and competition determine the routes by which matter and energy pass through ecosystems.
>
> —*Nelson George Hairston*

Biologist Elizabeth T. Odum expressed the same idea in a somewhat different way. She noted that "Everything belongs in an overall system and can be understood completely only in the context of the whole system."

In addition to the balanced interdependence found in nature, there were those scholars who felt it was equally important for young learners to understand the links that bind humans even more closely together through the interchange of their natural resources and manufactured goods. Panelist Teo Lye Huay from Singapore put it most simply: "People cannot survive without others." A historian on the opposite side of the planet commented:

> Whether we like it or not, we are faced with the coming together of the world. It has been taking place for some time and will continue. This means that [students] need to understand other cultures. No society can keep out the influence of other societies. Other cultures need to understand ours also. It also means that each country will and must change.
>
> —*Robert Byrnes*

In the same vein, Eleonora B. Masini, a faculty member at the Pontifical Gregoriana University in Rome, felt that "thinking in isolation is a luxury we can no longer afford," while a Thai academic,

Song-Sak Srikalasin, remarked on the need for ". . . cross-cultural sensitivity and global awareness" so that the young, as they move toward a new millennium, "can work together in greater harmony and with a greater appreciation of each other's strengths and limitations."

The threat of ecocide. The idea that irreversible damage may be done to the planet by spoliation and failure to recognize the interdependence of man and nature frequently surfaced among our panelists in both the natural and social sciences. "Ecocide is the destruction of the earth," sociologist Thomas Ford Hoult explained, and went on to say that "Our chance of saving humankind's one home will come only if we fully understand that we live in a closed ecosphere which we cannot continue to exploit unmercifully."

The problems created by environmental alteration were elaborated by an Indiana State geologist:

> Production and use of any mineral resource causes environmental alteration in some degree; most methods for improving the environment, or even avoiding environmental degradation, require consumption of mineral resources, especially fuels.
>
> —*John B. Patton*

Entropy and conservation. Along with a concern for the biosphere, one of the overarching ideas to come up quite frequently was the concept of *entropy*, a measure of "gone-ness." Readers with a scientific background will recognize that we are dealing here with the first and second laws of thermodynamics, a branch of physics developed in the last century. While energy can neither be created nor destroyed, it can be changed or degraded. For instance, when an automobile or a refrigerator is built, the raw materials used to make them take on a new form; and the original iron, copper, aluminum, and so on, is "gone." Hence our simple description associating entropy with "gone-ness."[5]

[5]My colleague at Indiana University, Gary Sojka, read our manuscript and made a point which helped me to clarify my own concept of entropy. He noted that: ". . . when discussing the first and second laws of thermodynamics and entropy you use an illustrative example involving metals and other raw materials, and finished manufactured goods such as automobiles and refrigerators. The analogy is formally correct and does illustrate the point. However, I'm afraid the lay reader may be confused by the examples. He may miss the concept of "goneness" because he will see that the raw materials are now in more organized, more "valuable" forms, i.e., consumer goods. It may be better to make the point by using a biological model. For example, assume a person eats an apple. The apple is a highly organized and potentially useful material. The entropy level in the apple is low. The person chews up the apple, digests it and ultimately oxidizes the constituent molecules down to the level of CO2. Entropy has now been greatly increased; 'goneness' has triumphed from the perspective of the apple. However, unlike most manufactured goods, much of the apple's former energy is now actually a part of the person who ate it."

The point made by a number of scholars is that young learners should understand that when 10 gallons of gasoline are used in an internal combustion engine, for all practical purposes they are transformed and cannot be restored to their original form.

As a physicist on our panel put it:

> Conservation of energy becomes valid under all conditions. It is an underlying thread of all science. Knowing fundamental laws of physics gives students a basis for solving problems rationally and [the] confidence needed to understand our world.
>
> —*Judith Rosenbaum Franz*

An additional point was made by physicist Roy Radha when he stated that "while the conservation of energy has to be understood in the context of a valid physical law, it also must be accepted as a valid [prescription] for [the] survival and growth of civilization."

The dangers of explosive population growth. A concern shared by many social and natural scientists was the inexorable increase in population growth, reviewed at some length in the previous chapter. This frequency with which this problem was mentioned suggests that it ranks with global interdependence as a concept that people of all ages everywhere need to understand and to seek to control.

The scientific method. While not of the same magnitude as the concepts of limits or of entropy, panelists in the natural sciences commented frequently on the scientific method. An interesting aspect of their comments was that they stressed both the importance of understanding the scientific method and the need to recognize its limitations.

The traditional view is that young learners should understand the two basic steps of the scientific method: 1) the initial formulation of hypotheses, 2) testing the hypotheses. In the elegant prose of Sir Peter Medawar, "All advances of scientific understanding, at every level, begin with a speculative adventure, an imaginative preconception of *what might be true*—a preconception . . . beyond anything which we have logical or factual authority to believe in. It is the invention of a possible world, or a tiny fraction of that world."[6] A somewhat different view was expressed by one of our panelists who flatly stated that:

> Students should understand that the so-called "laws of physics" are only man-made laws. They are nothing more than collections of known phenomena that have been classified and labeled.
>
> —*E. R. Laithwaite*

---

[6]Peter B. Medawar, *The Hope of Progress* (London: Methuen and Company, Ltd., 1972), p. 22.

Laithwaite also made the point that "students who seek [absolute scientific truth] waste their time."

Somewhat more temperately, Medawar contends that no beginning student in science should be led to believe that a given discovery such as the work of James Watson and Francis Crick on DNA depended on a given "right" method of inquiry and experimentation.

Panelists George Parks and Richard S. Westfall supported the "method of science" when they stressed the need for students to know how to "identify and approach new problems" and to understand "the scientific procedures by which science itself works." Other viewpoints which were expressed by both natural and social scientists include the following:

> You can't go from phenomena to underlying laws by the scientific method. Inspiration and genius are needed to do this.
>
> —*Donald Lichtenberg*

> There is a need for students to comprehend . . . that, particularly where humans are involved, much will be forever uncertain and unknowable.
>
> —*Phillip H. Abelson*

> Science . . . is different from other intellectual pursuits; it is never static; its theories are never final.
>
> —*William R. Breneman*

Again, most scholars appear to see the method of science as an important concept for our youth. It ranges from an initial working hypothesis to an eventual viable explanation of the unknown. But ultimate "truth" remains elusive, and some reports of scientific breakthroughs may actually conceal what went into their discovery by ascribing a "method" to it when in actuality it was a combination of human reason and luck!

Concepts from the Life Sciences

The life sciences include, for the purposes of our report, biology, zoology, physiology, anatomy, and botany, as well as such combination fields as microbiology, biophysics, or biochemistry. From interviews with scholars in these fields three major concepts frequently emerged: 1) the theory of evolution, 2) the unity of nature, and 3) the roles of photosynthesis and oxidation with respect to human existence. Let us examine these concepts and their implications for the future.

The concept of evolution. Scholars in the life sciences strongly urged that young learners grasp the concept of evolution. In the words of E. O. Wilson the theory of evolution by natural selection is crucial because ". . . it is generally recognized as the single unifying idea of biology, is profoundly important in Western thought, and, together with Marxism and Freudianism, is one of the several principal intellectual inventions of our culture made during the past two centuries."

Wilson's point was elaborated by Nelson G. Hairston in the following quotation:

> The premier concept of biology is evolution through natural selection. The full appreciation of this concept requires knowledge of all subsidiary concepts: heredity, physiology, population dynamics, behavior, and ecology. It is only through an understanding of evolution that biology makes sense. Yet natural selection is under attack, not only through bigotry, but from social scientists who might have to revise their cherished theories if they accepted the implications of evolutionary mechanisms.

Tracy Sonneborn was equally supportive of the theory because it "paints the grand picture of how matter has organized itself into more and more complex forms, starting with the inorganic and coming up to human beings."

A statement from microbiologist Gary Sojka carries the concept further:

> Biological evolution has not ended: It is a continuing process, and in fact we may be entering a period of extreme accelerated evolution. Some changes which may have taken millions of years through natural processes may now only take a Friday morning in someone's laboratory. One problem is that we will suddenly have enormously powerful techniques and tools that we don't have the institutions to handle.[7]

Not long after our interview with Sojka, newspaper headlines carried information about a controversial Supreme Court decision that permitted certain newly created life forms to be patented!

The question of whether humans have the wisdom to live with the power created by their scientific ingenuity has troubled persons working in both the physical sciences and in the life sciences. Scientific breakthroughs have given humans powers formerly ascribed to mythical deities. As a result of achievements in physics, of which nuclear energy is one practical outcome, many thoughtful people have expressed grave concern as to whether human judgment is capable of coping with such awesome powers. This uneasiness has deepened in the past two decades with the increasing sophistication in molecular

---

[7]For additional information see "The Miracles of Spliced Genes," *Newsweek*, 17 March 1980, pp. 62-71.

biology that is providing insight into the architecture of genetic codes. Moral and ethical issues are thus brought into direct confrontation with scientific achievement.

Pollution, test-tube babies, sperm banks, damaging the ozone layer with aerosol sprays, risking our lungs by inhaling asbestos dust, and divers scientific and technological developments leave us burdened with anxiety about the future. Our children need to be relieved from these anxieties. More explicitly, they need to see that developments in science can be a source of confidence and security, that many of our historic ills and problems such as smallpox are being alleviated by scientific developments.

The unity of nature. The basic laws of nature have an underlying unity. This concept was repeatedly mentioned by our panel of scholars. One of them, a zoologist, suggested that young learners need:

> . . . to be aware of the identity in all life, of the same genetic material and the same genetic code, that is, all the way from the simplest unicellular organisms up to the highest plants and animals.
>
> —*Tracy M. Sonneborn*

These concepts about diversity and uniformity are the essence of modern biologists' view of nature.

Panelist William Condon, a psychiatrist at Boston University, made the same point, but from a somewhat different perspective, when he said that students need "to acquire greater insight into the organization of nature. Nature is . . . both discrete-like and continuous simultaneously, and without contradiction." He also added that too much of modern science is "reductionist and fragmented" while life itself is a unity. A British physicist was even more specific:

> The analysis of matter into its constituent parts is not enough. Many important properties of matter, from electricity and viscosity to memory and intelligence, are consequences of the ways in which the parts of a piece of matter are arranged in relation to one another. The study of the emergence of properties out of structural arrangement is still in its infancy.
>
> —*Sir Alan Cottrell*

When we interviewed Sir Geoffrey Vickers, he gave us a copy of his paper, "Education in Systems Thinking."[8] In it he suggests how the

---

[8]Sir Geoffrey Vickers, "Education in Systems Thinking," Paper presented at the First International Meeting of the Society for General Systems Research in England, mimeographed. August 1979, 19 pp. Readers who are interested in his ideas should read his "Education in Systems Thinking," *Journal of Cultural and Educational Futures*, October 1979, pp. 2-8.

"unity concept" might be presented in a form appropriate to even primary school children. He points out how the school itself can be used as a model to help pupils understand that "the school is a [unified] physical system and is part of several physical support systems (water, sewage, electrical power and so on)." Also, "It is a social system, a career structure for teachers, as well as a way of life for children." Vickers concludes:

> From this complex yet familiar experience [of schooling] a series of studies could be drawn appropriate to all ages between six and sixteen, interesting in their own right, inviting contributions from all the familiar "disciplines" but focused not on these disciplines as such but on their use in understanding the [unity] of the real world. . . . Such a grounding . . . would help to prepare the next generation to live as responsible members of [the] many systems which make sometimes inconsistent demands on them and to discern and accept the limitations under which they and others act and need to act if they are to preserve the stability of the systems which sustain them.

Vickers is cited at some length because he was one of the relatively few scholars interviewed who had concerned themselves directly with the application of science concepts to elementary and secondary curriculum development that anticipates the future.

Photosynthesis, oxidation, and cycles in nature. Closely related to the concepts about the unity of nature were the repeated references made by the panel of scientists to the cycles in nature. Biologist W. Jackson Davis expressed it as the need to sense "how our lifestyles are imbedded within cycles of nature; for example, water, carbon, and nitrogen cycles." The working of photosynthesis and oxidation with respect to human existence was most often stressed. Here is a representative statement from a plant biochemist on our panel:

> The more children and youth know about the photosynthetic process and the effect of environmental factors such as salinity and temperature the better position we will be in to apply our knowledge as our normal food resources run out. . . .
>
> Energy supplies in the future depend on solar energy. Photosynthesis is the system which uses this energy. Photosynthesis is the most basic concept. It is the most important biology problem that students can look at since it is the basis for everything else. If there were not organisms which could use solar energy to make a fixed energy source [starch] then we, who are not capable of using this energy source, wouldn't survive. We can use this process to make not just food but chemicals and fuel sources. The future depends on good physical systems. The ability to facilitate those physical sys-

> tems may depend on how much we can know about the biological systems.
>
> —*Anthony G. San Pietro*

Davis, cited above, also expressed the opinion that a knowledge of the interactive processes of photosynthesis and oxidation is basic to the understanding of fuel cycles since fuel is obtained from photosynthesis and then converted to heat by oxidation.

Many of the scholars in the life sciences on our panel emphasized, in one way or another, the importance of building into the curriculum those concepts that will help youth to understand the importance of a balanced, man-to-nature relationship. The concepts of interdependence, evolution, population pressure, the acceptance of less extravagant lifestyles, and an emphasis on recognizing the unity of all living things, all lead to the conclusion that a more benign relationship with the environment is becoming a higher priority among the world community of scholars.

Concepts from the Physical Sciences

Many of the geologists, chemists, and physicists interveiwed stressed that young people need to understand the need to exercise caution in the uses made of their environment. As geologist Brian J. Skinner put it, "Man, in what amounts to uncontrolled experiments, has become a powerful geological agent capable of changing rates of erosion, affecting climate, and altering the natural fluxes of energy." Another geoscientist on our panel stressed the importance of understanding our vulnerability when it comes to nonrenewable sources:

> It is essential to the coming generation that children understand something of the nature, use, distribution and costs of obtaining the unrenewable resources. Energy, especially petroleum, is a good example of the type of problem arising from the lack of understanding of the general nature of oil. Other minerals are essential and are even less understood than is petroleum.
>
> —*Charles F. Park, Jr.*

Because of the severe harm being done to our planet, many scientists stressed that young people should acquire an understanding of those basic science concepts that are related to maintaining a reasonable standard of living throughout the world. Our panelists' recommendations for our young people varied from some knowledge of general science to quite specific information.

The listing below includes concepts mentioned by some of our panel of scholars that are important to young people.

Scholar	*Concept*
Judith R. Franz:	"The particulate nature of matter"
Donald Lichtenberg:	"Resources in general and energy in particular"
George A. Parks:	"Probability, as related to earth sciences, in order to make rational decisions"
Henry R. Mahler:	"The dynamic state of all cell constituents"
Richard H. Jahns:	"Plate tectonics which provides explanations for the origin, evolution, and present distribution of the earth's continents and ocean basins"
Henry R. Mahler:	"The concept that rocks in the earth tell the story of earth's long and complex history"
Roy Radha:	"The conservation of energy"

If youth are to make wise decisions in a science dominated, industrialized world, they must be exposed to more than rote learning of abstruse principles. Concepts such as "probability" or "conservation" can begin to be taught in a form that is understandable to most children at a very early age.

The Overlap of Natural and Social Science

Before turning to chapter 4 for the basic concepts in the social sciences, it is interesting to note areas of overlap expressed by the scholars in the various sciences. Four points were made repeatedly by our panel of scholars, points that were as likely to be voiced by an economist or anthropologist as by a physicist or geologist.

Human vulnerability. Scholars such as Ivor Davies and Lynton K. Caldwell pointed to the extreme vulnerability to which we are all exposed, for example, through an attack or manipulation by terrorists, by a nuclear holocaust, or by unwarranted aggression, both physical and psychological. "We need to reduce the vulnerability of the society we live in," said Caldwell, because, "Our society currently depends on everything working just right. We need, therefore, to examine the factors which cause our society to be vulnerable . . . ."

The need for more research. A second point made frequently was the need for the young to recognize the contributions of research and the need to support and extend it. Typical comments included:

> There is a need for a continuing, and ever greater, investment in scientific research. We need to study the conditions under which innovation is feasible.
>
> —*Lynton K. Caldwell*

> It is necessary to support financially the pursuit of basic or fundamental research—the addition to pure knowledge. Some of

> the most practical innovations have derived from disinterested research, research aimed at increasing human knowledge.
>
> —*Bernard I. Cohen*

> We must look upon research as a continuing effort at expanding the boundaries of knowledge, but not look upon science as a fixed body of truth to be learned and memorized. Rather we must see it as an ongoing enterprise.
>
> —*Richard S. Westfall*

Mass education; lifelong learning. One professor whom we interviewed had a bumper sticker on his car that read, "If You Think Education is Too Expensive, Try Ignorance!" This quip expressed the feelings of a number of participants in our inquiry both in the U.S. and abroad. In Scotland, L. C. Hunter spoke of the importance of "recurrent education"; in Paris, Guy Poquêt spoke of the need for lifelong education, which he referred to as "*êducation permanent.*" In Rome, Roberto Vacca urged extensive radio-television programming "on a massive scale and beamed toward every age level." Whatever the label or language used, there was little doubt that education for all, available throughout one's lifetime, was warmly endorsed.

When asked why lifelong learning was deemed to be so vital, Philip Abelson's response captured the thinking of many of our panelists: "Because of information overload, learners need sustained help in coping with the way in which knowledge is accumulating."

Information overload. Problems caused by the proliferation of knowledge was the fourth point made by many persons. It has been estimated that the knowledge generated in the 20th century exceeds that accumulated from all previous centuries! According to a specialist in linguistics on our panel, the graduates of our schools should be armed, insofar as possible, with information processing skills. These skills include language and interpretation skills as well as knowledge of how to process quickly the enormous eruption of new information which our culture provides.

Biophysicist John Platt made the same point, adding that "As the information available [to students] grows, they need to devise a rational and methodical approach to handling the content of articles, books, mail, and other media with which they are constantly bombarded." Bernard I. Cohen in the History of Science Department at Harvard also pointed out that the problem of overload was complicated in the sciences by the fact that knowledge today is forever in a state of flux and transition, hence "not final in any subject whatever!"

A French scholar, well known to students of the future, made another point which elaborated one way of coping with the challenge of overload:

> It is necessary to demystify science and knowledge, recognizing that all knowledge is subjective and that choices are, therefore, open to debate. More important than the mere transmission of information and knowledge is the development of [the learner's] capacities to reflect, comprehend, evaluate, and to coordinate [these capacities].
>
> —*Hughes de Jouvenal*

Concluding Comment

Science professor Isaac Asimov, best known for his science fiction and for his striking essays, recently made the comment that scientists tend to divide knowledge artificially and with "Greek-inherited snobbishness" into pure science and applied science.[9] He went on to say that the advance of knowledge of the physical world resides in the "coming together," in the interplay, of science and technology. As we close chapter 3 with its emphasis on the natural sciences and move to chapter 4 where the views of social scientists are summarized, Asimov's point about "coming together" is again appropriate to reiterate. Specialists in *both* realms have contributions to make to serve the world's good.

With the rapid changes that science and technology have brought and the resulting information overload, a comment made by Bentley Glass in 1968 is most appropriate as we look to accelerating curriculum change: "The educated man of yesterday is the maladjusted and uneducated man of today and the culturally illiterate misfit of tomorrow."

---

[9]In "Pure and Impure: The Interplay of Science and Technology," *Saturday Review*, 9 June 1979, pp. 22-28.

4

Basic Concepts: The Social Sciences

Man possesses, for a small moment in his history, the most powerful combination of knowledge, tools, and resources the world has ever known. He has all that is physically necessary to create a totally new form of human society—one that would be built to last for generations.

—D. L. Meadows, et al.

Weaving together the wide-ranging concepts of social scientists proved to be a formidable task! When categorizing the penetrating ideas from our interviews with social scientists, we found the same sort of cross-disciplinary overlap noted in chapter 3. Historians commented on economics, while economists referred to the lessons of history; and sociologists and anthropologists voiced their concerns with respect to economic trends or political problems!

In our interview with Sir Geoffrey Vickers, a notable contributor to our inquiry, he addressed himself to the reason for overlap. He noted, with respect to natural scientists, that their work has become more and more concerned with the total human environment. Furthermore, social anthropology, sociology, psychology, the science of communication, as well as economics, law, and political science are inherently concerned with the human condition.[1]

While the natural and social scientists differ in subject matter and their sources of knowledge, the body of tested knowledge which each gathers is of significance to all other sciences. As a result, information interchange inevitably leads to a continuous overlapping of ideas as well as to their cross-fertilization.

[1]For an elaboration of Sir Geoffrey's thinking, see his essay, "Science is Human" in *Value Systems and Social Processes* (Harmonsworth, Middlesex England: Penguin Books, 1970).

While we have explained the task of sorting out concepts in any given social science, the difficulty of doing so still remains. As in chapter 3, we will first look at some of the overlapping or cross-disciplinary concepts gathered from our interviews with social scientists. Then in subsequent sections we shall deal with concepts from each separate realm of social inquiry.

Cross-Disciplinary Concepts in the Social Sciences

The proliferation of knowledge, the speed of change. The need for youth and adults to understand the nature and the impact of the knowledge explosion that has occurred since 1940, as well as the prospect for continued rapid change, was repeatedly stressed by panelists. Usually this need was coupled with the need for learners of all ages to develop their "access skills;" for example, understanding information retrieval procedures, the role of computers, and library resources.

Panelist John Platt pointed out some years ago that since shortly before World War II global telecommunication had increased by a factor of 10 to become virtually instantaneous. Information processing during the same interval jumped by a factor of 10, while the speed of travel and increases in power from energy sources leaped upward by a factor of 10.[2] Some of our panel of social scientists felt that it was essential for youth to understand what exponential leaps in knowledge had wrought.

Learning how to learn. A natural development growing out of the increase in information is the need for learning how to learn. Said panelist Eugen Baer, "We need to understand that learning is a unique experience. Participation by individuals in this unique experience provides internal motivation for further learning." Other aspects of learning frequently mentioned by scholars on our panel included creative thinking, experimental inquiry, analytic skills, and knowledge-plus-process skills.

In 1961 the Educational Policies Commission defined the central purpose of American Education as follows:

> The purpose which runs through and strengthens all other educational purposes—the common thread of education—is the development of the ability to think. This is the central purpose to which the school must be oriented if it is to accomplish either its

---

[2]See Harold Shane, *The Educational Significance of the Future* (Bloomington, Ind.: Phi Delta Kappa Educational Foundation, 1973), pp. 39-40.

> traditional task or those newly accentuated by recent changes in the world.[3]

Some 20 years after the Commission completed its deliberations—years in which there was much dispute over the purposes of education—scholars once again endorsed the idea that students must learn to think. As mathematician Bruno de Finetti of Rome saw it, teachers should concentrate on heuristic or discovery approaches to learning rather than what he called "robothink." He said, "Young people should be encouraged to develop independently their unique or personalized approaches to problem solving [in mathematics] as opposed to adopting mechanistic, prescribed means to the solution of given problems." A representative comment from a French panelist was that:

> Our goals for education should not be to turn out cogwheels, but to develop in each child the richness of his humanity, potential for self-realization, and social skills. Or as Immanuel Kant said, to help him to achieve "all the perfection of which he is capable." The future challenges us to create an apprenticeship in acquiring an entirely new mode of thinking.
>
> —*Hughes de Jouvenal*

Ivor Davies added, "The basic skills of work require people to be *knowledge* workers rather than merely *skilled* workers. What knowledge workers know is not job-specific, but instead involves skills in diagnosing, exploring options, divergent thinking, making decisions, and evaluating."

Inquiry and analytical skills, not surprisingly, were endorsed by the social scientists just as understanding the methods of science was urged by our natural science panelists. British sociologist Earl Hopper recommended that students learn to distinguish between factual analysis and expressions of value; William R. Breneman urged that problems be approached *analytically* rather than *emotionally*. Emphasizing this point even more strongly, Jacob Fuchs stated, "The one overriding thing is to teach how to think analytically. Students must be able to analyze and reason rather than simply to memorize." Psychiatrist William Condon expressed a similar view by noting that an ability to reason "is basic in gaining an understanding of ourselves, of society, and of nature in general."

A concluding statement from a historian bluntly presents what it takes to learn how to learn. After remarking on the importance of ac-

---

[3]Educational Policies Commission, *The Central Purpose of American Education* (Washington, D.C.: The National Education Association, 1961), p. 12.

quiring a facility with books and learning how to read with understanding, he went on to say:

> One can understand [what is read] only when there is quiet and no movement. I think that today's youth are so accustomed to the frenetic pace of our automobile civilization, that they think everything can be done on the run. And I am especially distressed by their belief that it is possible to study with the accompanying noise of stereos and general ruckus.
>
> This is so damned evident in university dorms. Our major problem with today's high school graduates, when they come to the university, is their inability to anchor the seat of their pants to a chair and study quietly, for three or four hours at a time. If this idea could be put across in high school, it would be vastly helpful! The students have no idea of how they can waste time; they don't know how to organize their time.
>
> —*Robert H. Ferrell*

Understanding Systems

Systems analysis is a term used to describe the interrelationships of the functional components of anything (e.g., a school plant, a Neptune class nuclear submarine, or a new automobile model). A number of scholars recommended that students acquire a grasp of the systems approach, which is also known as "systems design," "systems engineering," or simply as "systems." As one panelist put it, "A systems approach does not inherently provide *answers*, but such an approach serves to insure that the necessary *questions* are asked."

According to a Canadian panelist:

> The systems approach enables the student to bring together ideas in different fields which, at first sight, might appear to be dissimilar but which, on examination, are found to suggest answers to the same kind of question. For example, in looking at economic growth we must ask, why grow? What kind of growth? These inquiries are at a different system level. These kinds of questions force us to look at different branches of knowledge since there is no accepted theory of economics which can deal with such questions.
>
> —*Walter H. C. Simmonds*

John Platt expressed the view that cybernetics, the science of effective organization, "can help us achieve our social, scientific, and educational goals. The [systems approach] allows us to follow a goal and, while looking for it, to correct errors, to anticipate future developments, and to continually readapt our plans." Platt also pointed out the importance of helping students become "aware of the various *levels* of systems: the individual, family, community, country, and world. If we are having trouble we should know how to approach this hierarchy to help solve our problems. Some decisions need to be made at higher levels of the hierarchy, others should be approached at lower levels."

When anthropologist Paul Bohannan was asked about basic concepts he said, "I believe that almost any concepts will do; it is the way they are put together that is of ultimate importance." Since the systems approach is designed to enable one to grasp dynamic, complex problems, its "ultimate importance" and value for learners resides in the way it helps them put things together.

The Need for Examined Values

Among the concepts that cut across all disciplines, the one most often mentioned or implied by social scientists (and by a number of natural scientists) was the need for students to develop a set of carefully examined values; especially, as Philip H. Abelson noted, "the old-fashioned virtues of self-discipline and an understanding of the Golden Rule." This concern with moral development appeared to be worldwide as the flavor of the following quotations from our panelists attests:

Richardo Diez-Hochleitner (Madrid): "Values are a necessary point of reference or basis for goals for students. The primary value is honesty, authenticity."

Kay Carmichael (Glasgow): "Many values . . . need to be reexamined. New values with regard to the changing status of families should be broached."

George Vaideanu (Paris): "Students should be aware of values . . . [and] understand the relation between national and universal values."

Rabbi Robert S. Hirt (New York City): "Man should strive to be moral, not merely rational. Man's own life and the world is *entrusted* to him, rather than *belongs* to him."

J. E. Hall-Williams (London): "Values need to be understood, and first among them is that of human life."

The Reverend Martin E. Marty (Chicago): "Students should be taught responsiveness and responsibility . . . for the development of [their] values, morals, and information."

Suthichai Wiengjayetz (Bangkok): "Rights and freedom should be accompanied by a sense of duty, as a good citizen, toward each person's own country and toward society as a whole. We need to see increased emphasis upon spiritual and other nonmaterialistic considerations."

An intriguing question can be inferred from this concern about values among scholars on our panel. This is the question of whether or not we have a ground swell of learned opinion that holds that the industrial world's high priority goal of accumulating more and more material goods must be rejected or at least tempered in the years ahead. Do many scholars now conclude that *less* as well as *small* is beautiful? Quite possibly, especially in the opinion of Dean Norman Henshey of McGill University who said, "Children and youth must be helped to avoid the 'neutron bomb' type of thinking which respects material things more than it respects people."[4]

Further evidence of the need to introduce new spiritual and moral values was seen in opinions of many of our panelists regarding the need for learners to see the relationships among such things as freedom and responsibility, equality, and respect for legal process.

Freedom, Responsibility, Equality, and Law

The issues surrounding freedom, responsibility, equality, and respect for the law were raised frequently in our interviews with such comments as "Students should understand equality and freedom and keep both in mind" (Luis Davila). "One should be aware of the sources of and kinds of ethical obligation and their relation to cultural history" (Sir Geoffrey Vickers). "The principle of responsibility, that one is accountable for his behavior, must be understood" (J. E. Hall-Williams).

A economist at Princeton made a rather detailed statement that bears on freedom, responsibility, equality, and law.

> A society cannot be free and stay free if it tries to enforce equality of wealth. [Students must understand that] people now use the word "equality" in terms of income or wealth. Historically this is wrong; equality means that you are not discriminated against or favored before the law.
>
> Young people should evaluate the concept that each person should get the same amount of everything. If wealth were equalized, it would have to be done again in ten years unless incomes were regulated also. If incomes were equalized, our economy would break down completely.
>
> Most of the world's problems are created by everyone wanting to get more. This creates animosity. People should work toward equality under law instead of for equality of income and wealth as a more desirable and feasible goal for the world's societies.
>
> —*Fritz Machlup*

---

[4]The controversial neutron bomb, developed in the 1970s achieves most of its lethal quality by its high radiation level which kills people, while doing relatively less damage to buildings and other structures.

Social commentator Vance Packard pointed out that responsible freedom can be achieved by our youth "only by considerable ingenuity, resourcefulness, and willingness to sacrifice in order to maintain a healthy, viable society." The same general sentiment marked the views of an educational columnist and sociopolitical writer of *The London Times.*

> Students should be aware of how our society is run and of the responsibilities and rights of the individual citizen. The internal politics of everything—from the local community to those of other countries and their interactions—should be understood so that future citizens will know how to take part in political decisions and how to change the system when change is desirable.
>
> —*Peter Wilby*

Concepts from History and Political Science

In 80 B.C. Cicero wrote that "not to know what happened before one was born is always to be a child." Not surprisingly, a number of historians made virtually the same point with respect to their field of specialization. But there were important, specific addenda for the Eighties. William H. McNeill represented the views of a number of respondents when he said, "Students should be aware of the history of *all* the world, not just the European-U.S. portion of the globe." Geoffrey Barraclough, former president of the British Historical Society, added that they also "should be aware of the relativity of their own culture in the whole span of world history."

Both Lawrence A. Cremin and Geoffrey Vickers commented on the role of time in our lives. Cremin's statement was as follows:

> With respect to the field of history, I would judge that it is important for children and youth to grasp an understanding of time in human affairs, of the fact that different sorts of individual and social change proceed at different rates, of change at different places and times, and of the stubborn persistence of certain human problems and concerns over the span of human history.
>
> —*Lawrence Cremin*

In addition to the time factor, Vickers emphasized the need for young people to become familiar with cultural history, a point which is elaborated later when the views of anthropologists are examined.

The panelists' concerns tended to cluster around several major concepts.

A sense of history. As historian Robert Byrnes points out, everyone must question, in historical perspective, their present personal values in order to sort out which of our established values should be and need to be preserved. Furthermore, each society must understand its past in order to evaluate its present as well as its future.

The degrees of democracy. That students should be aware that democracy is a matter of degree was suggested by Michael Marien, who went on to point out that we have a democratic form of government in the U.S. but far too little informed participation. The actual extent of popular rule varies from one country to another. In some places, for example, only males are enfranchised. Some democracies are socialist while others are capitalist. Human rights and economic opportunities also vary among democracies such as South Africa, Sweden, Britain, the U.S., and Mexico. Government by the people remains the exception rather than the rule.

Government-and-the-governed relationships. A specialist in urban development, Gordon Cameron, contended that the young people who are inheriting a responsibility for protecting and preserving democracy in such countries as Great Britain and the U.S. will have to rethink the nature of the relationship between government and the governed. In the recent past the government has been the major agent of change. In the future we can expect a fascinating battle between the government and at least some of the governed in a struggle to determine who will control the increasingly scarce public resources. Reflecting on his own country, Cameron noted that as the British people find that the government can do less and less for them, they will have to do more and more for themselves. The role of education, as he sees it, is one of helping citizens make enlightened choices and to understand the interrelatedness of decision making.

Centralized policy control and decentralized decisions. During the past 50 or 60 years in the U.S., power has tended to become more and more centered in the federal government. Students need to become familiar with the concept of centralized policy control and the strategies needed to preserve control by decentralized decision making.

Group efficacy in decision making. According to testimony from many of our interviews, young people need to learn the skills involved in achieving group efficacy. This is considered essential since many of our contemporary problems require group solutions. With the rapid growth of transnational interdependency there is a feeling that we have little or no power to control or to direct things that are happening. We have to overcome the growing sense of helplessness and restore the confidence that is a prerequisite for solving many national and international problems today. Arizona State University political scientist Henry Hinke sums up the situation: "Any viable constitutional government can continue to function only if there is adequate citizen involvement. Today there is too much apathy. We also need to restore a heightened sense of pride in our country."

Understanding the nature of power and national interests. Political scientists D. Latouche (Canada) and Alexander George (U.S.) both urged that the curricula of the 1980s and 1990s communicate to students the idea that "power" consists basically of human capabilities *plus* resources, rather than manpower and sophisticated weaponry. Therefore, there is a need, said Marvin Aliske, to convey through all levels of education that it is in the national interests to carefully husband all our resources (grain, technology, products, etc.) in order to maintain American ideals.

Probable sociopolitical developments likely to shape the world of tomorrow. Speculations regarding the future were made by a number of persons interviewed for this study. The following is a list of likely developments and trends provided early in our study by Lynton K. Caldwell, an Indiana University scholar, who summarizes with remarkable fidelity the views expressed by a majority of specialists in history and political science.

- The use of essential commodities as economic and political weapons to the disadvantage of the industrialized Western world and Japan has increased.
- Domestic problems as aspiration levels in Western democracies are increasingly threatened because their governments have not been able to deal effectively with shortages, inflation, recession, and unemployment.
- It is likely that transnational antagonism and terrorism will not diminish, and could increase.
- As the prospect of global crises increases, limited cooperation will occur among previously hostile nations with incompatible social, political, and economic goals.
- During the 25-year interval with which this study is concerned, no form of global government seems likely to emerge, although regional coalitions, by necessity, may increase.
- For the Western world there is the possibility that both personal freedom and social welfare policies may have reached a peak, or at least a plateau, after more than 200 years of progress.
- Western middle-class resentment and frustration stemming from loss of upward mobility may eventuate in radical self-protective political movements designed to replace democracy with a police state.
- The system of specialized agencies and cooperative regional programs developed by the United Nations offers the best approach

to attacking nonideological, worldwide problems that are responsive to applied science and technology.

• We have as yet found no way to accommodate the "revolution of rising human aspirations." The earth's limited carrying capacity and sociopolitical tensions will intensify as an anticipated population increase of between two and three billion occurs in the next two decades.

• The most successful governors of our interconnected planet in the period 1980-2000 will be those whose images of the future most nearly approximate reality and those who are least restrained in the vigorous exercise of carefully weighed survival tactics.

In view of the troubled future implicit in the 10 points above, it becomes of consummate importance for our schools, combined with all other educational resources, to help youngsters achieve a sense of "community," which is aptly defined by Robert Nesbit as:

> . . . relationships among individuals that are characterized by a high degree of personal intimacy, of social cohesion or moral commitment, and of continuity of time. All that is essential is that the basis be of sufficient appeal and of sufficient durability to enlist numbers of human beings, to arouse loyalties, and to stimulate an overriding sense of identity.[5]

Economics: "How Nice It Was Before Anyone Knew Anything About It!"

At a 1979 Indiana University conference, economist Kenneth Boulding commented, "How nice it was before anyone knew anything about economics," and then added that it was all right to make projections in the realm of economics "as long as you don't believe in them too much." Walter Heller, in his 1974 presidential address to the American Economics Association, also hinted at the fallibility of predictions when he told his fellow economists, "we have been caught with our parameters down."

While these comments from Boulding and Heller were obviously intended to be facetious, they do point up the rather confused state of current economic theory. Of all the natural and social science realms included in our inquiry, economics mirrored the widest differences of opinion among the scholars interviewed.[6] For this reason, fewer

---

[5]Robert Nesbit, *The Social Philosophers: Community and Conflict in Western Thought* (New York: Crowell & Company, 1973), p. 1.

[6]To savor the disagreement among the experts see "Prosperity without inflation" based on interviews with four Nobel Prize economists. *US News and World Report*, 15 December 1980, pp. 50-54.

concepts are included in this section. Some that are presented also tend to be opposing philosophical viewpoints; for instance, the growth doctrine versus the stable-state economy, or enlightened self-interest versus methodical redistribution of the world's material goods.

Free enterprise and enlightened self-interest. Panelists John Mee, Fritz Machlup, and J. Richard Aronson wanted to be sure that U.S. youth clearly understood the virtues of the free enterprise system.

> A better understanding of the free enterprise system should help the next generation avoid false expectations and disappointment. They should perceive it as an economic institution based on voluntary exchange among individuals; one that is often, although not always, capable of generating economic results that are both efficient and fair. For allocating resources and making decisions about a whole set of goods and services, free enterprise is the best way yet that we have thought of to match people's wants with the system's capability to satisfy them.
>
> —*J. Richard Aronson*

Mee added that young Americans should be aware of "intelligent selfishness" or the "enlightened self-interest" concept; namely, that to get what you want from someone, you have to give in return something which that person wants. At the same time, as Stanley M. Elam noted while reading a first draft of this manuscript, the rubric "free enterprise" should not be used to defend such knavery as sweatshops in the garment industry or in migrant farming areas where owners profit from the "sympathy of government inspectors who won't enforce minimum wage laws designed to protect the worker."

Trade-offs. One of the two most frequently mentioned basic concepts in the field of economics (the other was economic equity) was the trade-off. As one of our economist panelists put it:

> This concept goes way beyond economics. It is of vital importance to so many public policy issues and private choices that it should be learned at an early age! Some cases in point are the trade-offs: a) between reduction of inequality of income and wealth and incentives to work, save, and invest; b) between lower levels of employment and higher rates of inflation; and c) between pressing energy needs—especially from coal and uranium—and pressing environmental needs such as protecting air and water.
>
> —*Walter Heller*

Similar comments were made by scholars from widely separated locations such as Thailand (Suthichai Wiengjayete), North Carolina (Duncan Macrea, Jr.), Indiana (George W. Wilson), and Arizona (John Cochran). For example, after reiterating the familiar phrase, "There is no such thing as a free lunch," Aronson commented: "Students should know there must be trade-offs. They should not fall victim to the 'wishing syndrome,' the romantic notion that one simple solution to a problem will solve everything without . . . repercussions in other areas."

Economic equity. Although many of the panelists discussed the need for youth to grasp the principles of economic equity, opinions varied widely as to suitable cures for contemporary inequities. On the one hand we find University of London sociologist Tessa Blackstone advocating that students understand the notion of and the need for redistribution of the world's goods because of "the large inequalities which exist within industrial societies, and the even greater differences between industrial and underdeveloped societies," a liberal view with which another London scholar, Yogini Janki agreed strongly.

A Swedish scholar at the University of Stockholm was more explicit.

> The key concept in the controversies permeating the highly industrial and post-industrial societies is equality—both as it is interpreted philosophically and the way in which it is translated into social action. But does it mean equality of *opportunity* or equality of *results*? Does it imply *uniformity* or *diversity* of treatment and of living conditions?
>
> —*Torsten Husén*

Boris Kluchnikov, professor of economics at the University of Moscow, currently on leave at Unesco as director, Division of Educational Policy and Planning, responded to Husén's second question by urging that diversity rather than standardization be emphasized in instructional practice. Uniformity, he felt, should not be sought and could not be attained because of individual differences.

Fritz Machlup tended to be more cautious, and Henri Janne, sociologist at the University of Brussels, emphasized understanding others rather than arguing for an egalitarian redistribution of wealth. "Students should be prepared to have a dialogue with other people without discrimination or limits. This implies being able to put themselves intellectually and morally in the situation of others. That is the basis of good social systems and peace."

Several economists in addition to Machlup questioned whether young learners should be taught that a significant redistribution of the world's goods, as Blackstone urged, was desirable. As one European panelist noted off the record, "People in the 'have-less' group, as I've come to know them (in Europe and Asia), will never be satisfied with equality. They seek the preferential status of the 'have-mores'. Rulers in the oil-rich Middle East are already learning that the appetite [of their people] for consumer goods increases geometrically when their lifestyles are doubled arithmetically. Redistribution is a dream, too, because there will never be enough Euro-American style affluence to go around."

Understanding diverse economic goals. In a discussion of alternative economic futures a pertinent point was made by the Soviet economist Kluchnikov. What young learners are exposed to with respect to economics obviously depends on whether one is thinking in terms of communist or capitalist ideology. One decides what concepts should be taught on the basis of national economic goals, which appear at present to be difficult to reconcile insofar as the Soviet Union and the U.S. are concerned.

From growth to dynamic equilibrium. In a preliminary report of this study presented at a Unesco symposium in Paris in July 1980, the writer used the model in figure 3 to summarize basic developments in industrialized world economics during the next several decades that seem important for all learners to grasp.

From the beginning of the industrial age, as suggested by the cone-shaped portion on the left side of the model, the growth doctrine was widely accepted, and probably reached its greatest degree of acceptance in the period between 1946 and 1970. Since publication of the pioneering Club of Rome report, *The Limits to Growth* in 1973, there have been numerous publications and pronouncements telling us that we must adjust our lifestyles to meet planetary problems of pollution, resource depletion, and the like—problems so familiar to readers as to require no additional comment here.

As we begin to come to grips with the constraints imposed by limited resources, presumably a more stable state will begin to take form during the 1980s, one in which conservation, recycling, and frugality become far more widely practiced than they are at present. Section III of the model, labeled "stable state," suggests an emergent trend toward ecologically sound economic and social policies. Between 2000 and 2006, the U.S. and world economy might well encounter an interval of "dynamic contraction" (Section IV) when humans cut back on material consumption. "Dynamic contraction" is not a euphemism for indicating sharp cutbacks or retrenchment in planetary life-styles. Rather, as Noble Prize winner Dennis Gabor phrased it, "We must work toward a mature society, stable in numbers and in material production, in ecological equilibrium with the resources of the earth."[7] In such a time when humans seek to do more

[7]Dennis Gabor, *The Mature Society* (New York: Praeger and Company, 1972). p. 170.

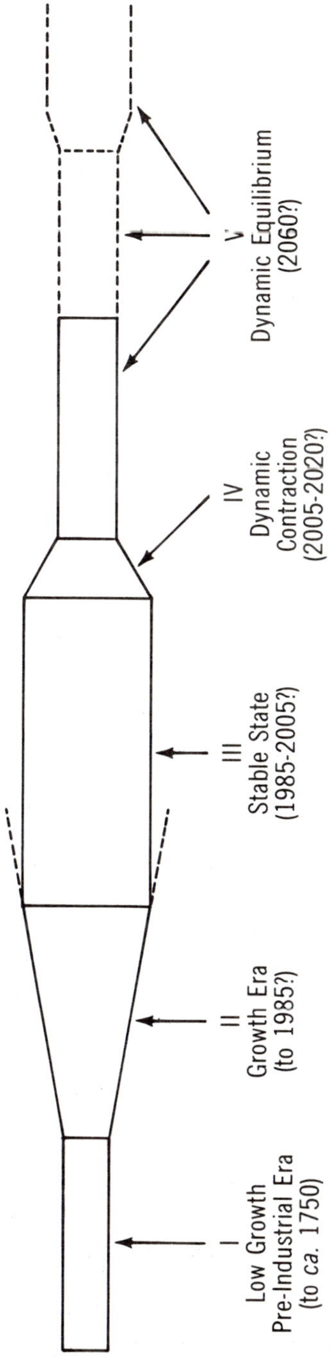

Fig. 3. Growth, stability, dynamic contraction, and dynamic equilibrium (not to chronological scale)

with less: 1) excellence would replace quantitative growth, and 2) possession would tend to supersede conspicuous consumption. The first is advice to the industrial elite, the second to everybody, according to Gabor.

One hopes that the elimination of waste in the period labeled "dynamic contraction" in the model will be followed by an era of what Gabor calls "dynamic equilibrium." Section V of the model represents a period that, perhaps 50 years hence, will eventuate in improving standards of living, but without today's conspicuous waste and swanky garbage, with increased supply and production instead of escalating demand and consumption.

Sociology: Toward a Global Community

Global community. Kay Carmichael, a senior lecturer in social administration and social work at the University of Glasgow, contended that "students need to be informed about where our society is moving. Currently schools emphasize the past. A good place to start would be to inform them about the present situation." From our interviews, most sociologists and such social commentators as Vance Packard and Aurelio Peccei would agree with her. Peccei, for instance, stated that young learners ". . . should know that human society is now a global society which needs new forms of mutual comprehension and solidarity on a global scale." Similar comments regarding the development of a sense of membership in a "community of humankind" were also expressed by the political scientists and historians in our survey.

Other concepts mentioned frequently included: the importance of local solutions as prerequisites to solving global problems; mobility and urban sprawl; the trend toward an "information economy"; the dangers of social fragmentation; and the need for voluntary simplicity and frugality. Each of the concepts will be considered briefly.

Local solutions as prerequisites to global problem solving. Ricardo Diez-Hochleitner, Director of the Fundación General Mediterrânea in Madrid, made a comment that expressed the sentiments of a number of participants in our interviews. "Global problems will be solved only by starting at the local level. Well-being is not simply the result of progress but rather it is related to a feeling of dignity of life, of rewarding human relationships." Diez-Hochleitner's concluding statement seemed especially relevant to the present inquiry: "The educational system which the future demands must be based on the knowledge that what young people are looking for is not merely a job or money but rather the criteria for successfully facing life."

Such widespread interest in "thinking globally but acting locally" led the World Future Society to chose this theme for its 1980 conference in Toronto.[8]

Mobility and urban sprawl. Three of our panel of international scholars eloquently presented the case for informing students of the social consequences of mobility and sprawl. Gordon Cameron, an urban planner at the University of Glasgow, felt that the current practice of allowing cities to spread will soon come in for critical reexamination. Laurence L. Waters pointed out that "Students should be aware of the increased mobility of populations all over the world, with a resulting impact on social structures, particularly on family life. This has led to many special problems and challenges for people of all ages as they strive to adapt to the collision of cultures and various environmental problems."

Sir Geoffrey Vickers, who has spent considerable time on urban problems, directed our attention to a British report on the topic which said in part:

> . . . urban traffic consists of journeys which begin or end at urban buildings and which are generated by activities in those buildings. Thus the traffic is a function of the buildings. Buildings in towns need the accessibility which is required by the activities which they generate. If these activities clog the roads with traffic, the resultant mess is a symptom of a deeper problem, the problem of providing urban buildings with accessibility.[9]

With this statement, Vickers illustrated how the "seamlessness," the interrelatedness of everything, needs to be made clear to the learners if they are to function successfully in society.

The information economy. Canadian panelist Kimon Valaskakis of the University of Montreal discussed at considerable length what students should understand about the sociological implications of the emerging "information economy." An information economy is one in which workers (often replaced by electronic devices) are involved in the encoding and decoding of data and information retrieval. It is an economy that uses television, computers, and home-linked satellites to create what one scholar called a "wired planet." It is an economy for a world where electronic banking, electronic office and school work, electronic voting, and even electronic house calls (using tele-

---

[8]See Frank Feather, ed., *Through the 80's: Thinking Globally, Acting Locally,* (Washington, D.C.: World Future Society). In particular see papers prepared by Willis W. Harman, Roy Amara, and other authors of Part II, "A Global Perspective."

[9]C. Buchanan, *Traffic in Towns*, Report of the Steering Group and Working Group appointed by the Minister of Transport (London: HMSO, 1963).

vision and special monitoring devices to check vital signs such as blood pressure) become a reality.

> A key factor in the next 20 years will be the evolution of the economic system toward an *information* economy and away from an *industrial* economy. An information economy is one where the principal source of value is the transformation of information rather than the transformation of goods. Some effects of an information economy will be noticeable in labor, in the location of economic activity, energy trade-offs, and in politics.
>
> —*Kimon Valaskakis*

There are a number of implications for education in the developing information economy that now employs over 40% of the U.S. work force. These implications include widespread instruction in computer science, greater use of self-instructional materials, and new approaches to meeting new vocational needs through education.[10]

Social fragmentation. Both sociologists and specialists in other fields expressed concern about the increasing Balkanization of America—the problem of proliferating subgroups promoting special interests to the detriment of the general welfare. A representative expression of this concern follows:

> The major ailment of our society today is social fragmentation arising from high mobility and family disruption. It is important for our youth to recognize and to strive to overcome this fragmentation. Among other things, we must work in our neighborhoods to develop not only a greater sense of community but a feeling of continuity.
>
> —*Vance Packard*

Voluntary frugality versus enforced austerity. One last point made in various ways by panelists was that Western industrialized society was facing a choice between *voluntary* frugality and *enforced* austerity in the next several decades. As Canadian panelist Dean Norman Hanshey phrased it, "Students must understand *now* the importance of voluntary simplicity—of 'decluttering' future lifestyles—lest government-directed austerity be the alternative 20 years hence."

One is reminded of a statement made in the 1920s by Calvin Coolidge when he said that people should "wear things out, patch things up, make things do." If the industrial age is waning, if it is entering a state of transformation rather than one of ecologically prudent re-

---

[10]For further insight into the information economy and electronic break-throughs see "The Robot Revolution," *Time*, 8 December 1980, pp. 72-83 and "What the Next 20 Years Hold for You," *U.S. News and World Report*, 1 December 1980, pp. 51-55.

industrialization as Alvin Toffler, Jackson W. Davis, and others contend, Coolidge's maxim may once again find acceptance. Conceivably, prudence and thrift will supersede the extravagance and waste of what Toffler has characterized as a "throw-away society" in his book *Future Shock*.

Anthropology: The Human Riddle

An important contribution of 20th century anthropologists is the concept that the culture in which individuals live has a profound influence on their overall behavior.[11] As an anthropologist panelist put it:

> The concept that ties anthropology to education and vice versa is that people learn differently in different cultures—coupled with the concept that their reinforcement schedules are different. Few educators seem to operate according to these precepts even though they may know them intellectually. The notion that people are more concerned with controlling their inputs than with anything else is also crucial to the understanding of intercultural communication in any setting.
>
> —*Edward T. Hall*

Paul Gebhard in his interview elaborated on the point. "Students need to adopt an attitude of toleration based on an understanding that there is a great variation in human needs and feelings. The notion of great variation among humans also can be applied to cultural differences. Furthermore, tolerance, situational ethics, and an understanding of cultural relativism help us to cope with change. This does not mean, of course, that people should accept everything [in other cultures]."

James V. McConnell and Reynold Ruppe made the same point, namely, that culture permeates human behavior. While thoughts, feelings, and actions have biological correlates that cannot be ignored, McConnell points out that people also must recognize how strongly we are influenced by sociocultural inputs. "Unless we realize the power of these inputs on our behaviors and emotions," he concluded, "we will never acquire enough knowledge about ourselves to maximize our potential."

Lynton K. Caldwell spoke of the importance of cross-cultural and transdisciplinary insights. He argued that if students were to understand the wellsprings of human behavior, then the gap between the biological and social sciences needed to be closed. "Practical experi-

---

[11] This thesis was advanced convincingly by Edward T. Hall in *The Hidden Dimension* (Greenwich, Conn.: Fawcett Publications, 1959), pp. 9-13.

ences [also] are needed to verify some of the assumptions we hold. . . . If we are to avoid serious political and social conflicts in the future, we have to take psychological, sociological, anthropological, and biological insights into account."

Understanding cultural pluralism: culture and compromise. According to Robert St. Clair we need to develop in our students an understanding of and appreciation for cultural pluralism; but "We also should help them become aware of the role of compromise," a point also made by George Bozzini. As Bozzini sees it: "Students should understand the nature of cultural compromise, and they should expect others to learn to compromise, also. If we are going to make progress in solving world problems, everybody has got to give in some of the time."

Attitudes and modes of thought as learned behaviors. John Hudson, Thomas F. Hoult, and Albert Bandura were among the scholars who felt that behavior and attitudes are acquired through the process of experience.

> Behavior is learned. It is neither inherited nor is it unchangeable. The implications of this concept are profound. When we meet people who are different, we must realize that they have *learned* behaviors different from ours. Attitudes also are *taught.* The way we are taught to think about the world we live in and about the people with whom we interact is the critical factor in our behavior.
>
> —*John Hudson*

The case for foreign language. Both anthropologists and scholars in other disciplines repeatedly affirmed the crucial importance of a command of at least one second language. As L. L. Waters saw it, the neglect and decline in second language instruction will "leave the U.S. with more cross-cultural problems than ever." Luis Davila stressed an additional language as an important factor in identifying with those in other cultures and understanding other countries. Eugen Baer envisioned "communicative competence" as essential for transdisciplinary, transcultural, or transethnic understanding. Such skills, he felt, were especially crucial for bringing about "a faster adaptation to rapidly changing situations in all spheres of life."

Linguistics scholar Robert St. Clair advocated that a cultural approach be taken in teaching a second language: "Nonverbal communication—semiotics should also be stressed. We use language as a probe to test people—to ascertain whether they can communicate with us. . . . We create assumptions and expectations and make errors due to language misconceptions."

St. Clair's reference to semiotics needs elaboration. Semiotics is a technical term that refers to the study of patterned human behavior with respect to communication in all its moods and modes. Thomas Sebeok also was a proponent of improving students' concepts and skills in the field of semiotics. Since the need for improved communication was a theme that was developed by one panel member after another, there can be little doubt as to the importance of semiotics in the curriculum.

Et Passim . . .

In this chapter we have attempted to categorize the basic concepts that social scientists feel are essential for survival in the future. There were other concerns expressed that do not lend themselves to neat categorization. Several persons spoke of the need for students to appreciate the value of periods of reflection and tranquility, of solitude and silence, and perserverance in the absence of instant gratification. Another cluster of respondents spoke out on the importance of "some notion of excellence"; of content-mastery and self-mastery—as James Ross MacDonald put it, for those "working out to the edge of knowledge and then expanding the known."

Sally S. Shelley and Robert Muller, both at the UN, expressed the hope that students learn about concepts pertaining to the importance of peace in an era in which sophisticated weapons made war no longer a way of solving human differences. Said Shelly, "Loyalty to country does not and should not preclude loyalty to the human race as a whole." As two panelists from the United Kingdom put it, "We must get young people to accept an apprenticeship in the affairs of society so that they get inside what's going on and become involved in the struggles to reform society and inculcate humanistic skills, nontechnological skills—those skills exclusive to humans—which cannot be performed by machines. . . ."

Conclusion: The Restoration of Values

In rereading chapters 3 and 4 it began to dawn on the project staff that many of the concepts, principles, and values repeatedly mentioned had a flavor that seemed very familiar; a tantalizing *déja vu* quality! For several hours one of the writers sifted through brittle old pamphlets and dusty books seeking the points that had long ago appeared in print. Finally several remarkably prescient vintage essays by educational writers were found.

Prescience from the past. Before identifying the authors of these essays and revealing their publication dates, let us present a synthesis of the points which were made in their yellowing pages.

1. Man, under the guidance of his intellect, can create better tomorrows.

2. Science has freed humans from subordination to supermundane powers by giving them an "open universe . . ."

3. Biologically, humans are multipotential. They may become one of many things, or nothing at all.

4. The dignity, worth, and independence of humans is threatened by the massiveness of a technoscientific civilization—threatened socially, economically, and politically.

5. [Scientific] laws are human constructions, not pictures of reality. The universe is in a state of "becoming," not in a state of being. All "laws" are approximate.

6. Change in the learner is wrought through changing the environment, not by mere indoctrination, command, or direction.

7. Education does not merely *permit* intelligence to express itself, it *creates* intelligence as a dam creates water power.

8. Learners are dynamic organisms, not atomistic responding mechanisms. They are integrated organisms, not bundles of conditioned reflexes. Human beings are more than a summation of their extant parts, and the whole determines the activity of the parts.

9. The individual is an energy system in unstable equilibrium. Disturbed equilibrium → tension → motivation → action → greater stability → disturbed equilibrium and so on *ad infinitum*.

10. The essence of the learning process is discovery, a continuous doing-of-something-new. Learning stems from creative thinking; each task, when mastered, is a creative adventure in discovery.

11. The meanings of ideas or conceptions are to be found in the behaviors and practices to which they lead.

12. Changes wrought in individuals as a result of their experiences denote education.

13. Experimental inquiry is the supreme criterion for decision making.

14. "Mind" is a quality of behavior, a function. The learner is part and parcel of the course of events. Mind manifests itself in the conduct of the individual. The learner acquires "mind," a rational nature, as the meaning of environment is mastered.

15. Thinking, the reflective act, a) begins with a situation of difficulty, b) develops through observation, data gathering, and the tracing of implications; until c) a problem is defined, d) a plan of action has been projected, and e) it eventuates in action that tests the plan.

16. An effective education replaces passive, rote learning with a form of active community life within the school and involves vital interaction with the surrounding natural and social environment.

17. It is by participating in the activities of a society that the learner acquires the behaviors characteristic of selfhood.

18. Each society insures its own continuance and well-being through the education of learners of all ages.

19. Democracy embodies the principle that each individual possesses intrinsic worth and dignity. Individuals enjoy the status of *ends* and institutions the status of *means*.

20. A sound education supports the concept of a *planning* (not a *planned*) society in which resources and production are governed democratically for the good of all. It is a supreme task of education to bring about this social transformation.

A careful examination of the views of many participants in our interviews reveals that they bear a remarkable similarity to the 20 points made above! Equally interesting is the fact that the first 10 are a summary of certain writings from L. Thomas Hopkins or from Orville G. Brim's 17-page essay, *The Foundations of Progressive Education*, published in 1935 at Ohio State University. Points 11 through 20 are synthesized from a Progressive Education Association pamphlet prepared in the 1930s by John L. Childs for purposes of presenting some of the educational implications of John Dewey's writings.

Since these 20 points are so similar to the opinions of the scholars whom we surveyed, we might ask if we are on the threshold of a restoration of neglected educational principles and values needed for survival. Probably so. Furthermore, if this conclusion is correct those proponents of an open but substantive, liberating, humanistic curriculum have found powerful intellectual allies among the ranks of today's widely respected natural and social scientists.

Education for a new millennium, in an era of tension and turmoil, seems to be emerging as a lifelong process designed to make humans of all ages more receptive to those values that have guided civilization since long before the time history remembers. Such human values include appreciating, understanding, and creating beauty and personifying truth and integrity in thought and action. As Alfred North Whitehead said in the 1920s, "What we should aim at is producing [humans] who possess both culture and expert knowledge in some special direction."[12]

Assuming that the overarching goal of education is to preserve, extend, and improve human values, one might ask, what is an educated person? Both the prescience of the past and present testimony from scholars, suggest that an educated person is one in whom the latent powers of the human mind have been set free. Such a person knows how to apply knowledge wisely in the context of sound values.

---

[12]Alfred North Whitehead, *The Aims of Education* (New York: New American Library, Mentor Education, 1949), p. 13.

No longer a member of a small elite, the educated person in a new millennium will value human achievement, whether it emanates from the mind or the hands. The educated person will have learned the meanings of social responsibility in the protection of human rights and will understand that possessions bring social duties, and opportunities create obligations. One can hope that the educated person will understand and use the techniques that make democracy work. Further, educated persons will use the skills and knowledge that can make them productive people who are useful to themselves and to the larger world community. Finally, educated persons will need to comprehend the meaning of ethical, interpersonal relations; to have faith in and respect for others, irrespective of their ethnic and cultural antecedents; and to have faith in themselves and in their destiny.

Since this seems to be the message in our project interviews, it now becomes important to ask what kind of *schooling*, what kind of lifelong *education*, what sort of *learning* experiences are to be sought as we begin to make what Guy Poquêt termed "the long-range social and educational decisions which will shape tomorrow's world." It is with these questions that Part II of our report is concerned.

II

Learning for a New Millennium

5

Creating a Curriculum That Anticipates Tomorrow

Societies, like landscapes, are remodeled by two types of processes. One of them is cataclysmic: the revolutionary upheaval which like an earthquake or volcanic eruption, rearranges the whole scene with spectacular suddenness. Such apocalyptic events don't occur often, though, so waiting for the revolution can get to be as tedious as waiting for the next ice age; and when it comes, the results are likely to be unpredictable.

The other process is one of slow accretion—the way coral builds an island or algae transform a tidal estuary, over centuries, into dry land. In like fashion the social landscape changes constantly—if almost imperceptibly—as the consequence of innumerable small acts and innovations . . . .

—John Fisher, "The Easy Chair,"
Harper's Magazine, October 1971

The views expressed by a number of scientists in our earlier chapters suggest that we may be on the threshold of major changes in industrial societies that, as John Fisher tells us above, can rearrange the world we have known with spectacular suddenness. However, neither his descriptions of revolutionary upheavals nor of very gradual change seems to fit the conditions for curriculum development that anticipates the future. Revolutionary approaches to changes in educational practices could easily result in chaos. Conversely, glacial changes are likely to increase even further the lag in meeting social needs for which the traditional curriculum has sometimes been blamed. Where, then, can we turn to find guidelines for developing a curriculum that anticipates the demands likely to be placed on all learners in the years ahead?

In order to speculate about this question, and because of its relevance for curriculum change, let us turn to Thomas S. Kuhn's influential paradigm pertaining to the structure of scientific revolutions.[1]

Scientific Revolutions and Curriculum Changes

Kuhn's paradigm. Using illustrations such as the replacement of Ptolemy's geocentric solar system with a Copernican heliocentric view of the universe (made possible by the invention of the telescope), Kuhn pointed out that when anomalies are noted in an old paradigm, a crisis ensues.[2] As a result, new paradigms are proposed; conflicting ideas battle for ascendancy; and eventually an idea or concept wins out and replaces the discredited one. How this works is explained in more detail in figure 4.[3]

Curriculum development and societal change. By using Kuhn's model of changes in the field of science, we can construct an analogous paradigm to illustrate the nature of evolutionary curriculum changes derived from our emerging images of the future.

Let us begin by recognizing the obvious: Curriculum development is directly influenced by changes in U.S. society and the societal transitions that accompany them. As we contemplate educating for a new millennium, it is vital that all professionals concerned with curriculum have an understanding of evolutionary changes in the content and practice of instruction which can be derived from our images of the future.

From yesterday to tomorrow. As we explore the interaction between curriculum development and societal change, it is helpful to recall certain instructional and curricular practices of 20 to 40 years ago, which are analogous to the "old paradigms" used in our visualization of Kuhn's structure of scientific revolutions. These practices were often associated with one-teacher, self-contained classrooms in the six-year elementary school. A two- or three-year junior high program was followed by a three- or four-year high school. In the last six years instruction was largely subject-centered with a departmental organization in the basic fields of mathematics, science, foreign language,

---

[1]See Thomas S. Kuhn, *The Structure of Scientific Revolutions, 2nd ed.* (Chicago: University of Chicago Press, 1970).

[2]Kuhn defines paradigms as "universally recognized scientific achievements that for a time provide model problems to a community of practitioners." He also notes (p. 10) that paradigms share two characteristics: 1) they are sufficiently unprecedented to attract an enduring group of adherents and 2) are also sufficiently open-ended to create all sorts of problems for practitioners to resolve.

[3]Kuhn, to the best of my knowledge, described his paradigms verbally and never attempted a graphic representation such as appears in figure 4. Jack Wilson, while one of my students, suggested the original sketch, which has been modified and reproduced here. HGS

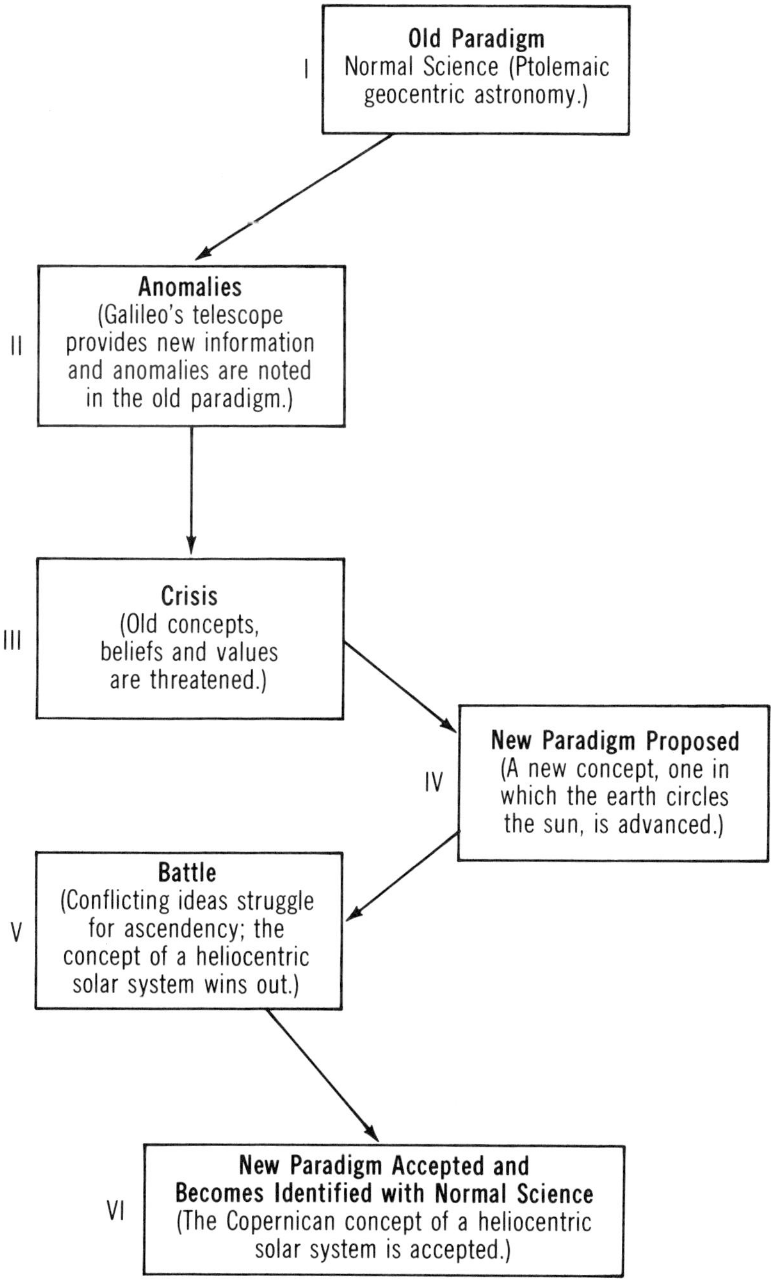

Fig. 4. The structure of scientific revolutions

English, and history. Often, in grade eight, it was common practice to have boys assigned to wood or metal shop and girls to home economics.

High school programs usually streamed young leaners into college preparatory, business/secretarial, or general vocational courses. Dramatics, sports, hobby clubs, and other extracurricular activities were usually available at both the junior and senior high levels.

Quite often the secondary school facility was new, while junior high youth inherited an aging hand-me-down high school building because of the enrollment increases during the years following World War II. Elementary school children fared better with respect to school housing. Because there were so many of these youngsters, much new construction had to be undertaken to house them.

The curricular and organizational practices briefly described above reflected a few aspects of the changing social order. In addition to such social indicators as demographic trends showing shifts in U.S. age distribution, there were other indications of future developments in taxation, productivity, family size, the drug culture, youth crime rate, social welfare programs, balance of trade, gross national product, and others.

Social indicators presage major transitions in a given way of life. They have proved to be fairly reliable means, when interpreted with care, of forecasting future developments in our society. Nevertheless, in the past, most of us have had considerable difficulty envisioning future developments. For instance, many Americans, if asked to speculate about the aerospace program in 1960; would have failed to foresee its long-range influence on U.S. life. Few would have anticipated the way in which highly sophisticated computers would affect our lives in such ways as monitoring income taxes, supporting credit card empires, reservng a specific seat for a Chicago-Los Angeles flight, or checking the blood chemistry of a patient in the hospital.

The point of this discussion of societal transitions and the curriculum is that educators need to study contemporary social indicators that anticipate the future and begin to design learning experiences that will enable young people to live effectively in the technological, economic, and social futures that are pressing upon us.

The Interaction of Social Indicators and the Curriculum

Curriculum planning, while respecting the contributions of our broad cultural heritage, also needs to be guided by indicators of probable futures. An example helps to make the point clear. One of the significant social indicators of the past two decades has been the successful entry into the U.S. labor market of millions of women, a large number of whom still have children of school age. This phenomenon has had a wide-ranging effect: changing the nature of home life, increasing competition among teenagers and males for jobs, and permitting greater personal freedom and mobility among female wage earners.

As Ralph W. Tyler pointed out in a conversation with one of the writers, "In 1960, 26% of mothers of school age children were in the labor force; in 1974 this figure had climbed to 51%. . . . Many children now return to homes in which they have very little guidance, and this creates new responsibilities for other educational agencies." Six years later, in 1980, the number of women in the world of work had reached 62% and one-third of this large group had children who were five years of age or younger! Clearly, such a development is a social indicator that suggests the need for the curriculum to reflect a greater awareness of and provisions for early childhood education.

An evolutionary curriculum change paradigm. Our adaptation of Kuhn's paradigm in figure 5 is designed to illustrate the structure of evolutionary changes in education, changes that are neither cataclysmic upheavals nor glacially slow. It should help educators to phase into the curriculum the survival concepts which our study sought to identify. The paradigm illustrates how conventional curriculum and instructional practices (I) are destabilized or made obsolete by trends and forces that are first reflected in social indicators (II); and then, as major social changes (III) emerge, it becomes necessary to reform our instructional content and methods.

The split between the defenders of the status quo curriculum and the proponents of innovations that social transitions require eventually leads to crises (IV) in education. Such crises occurred when writers such as Rudolph Flesch and Arthur Bestor in the 1950s or John Holt and Jonathan Kozol in the 1960s launched their attacks on the schools. Bestor, for instance, was voicing his concern over the loss of academic skills that create what he called the "educational wastelands" or a retreat from the essentials or basic learning.[4] Holt and Kozol, described by William Van Til as the "compassionate critics," began in the late 1960s to express concern about the lack of humane concern for young learners.

Continuing with the paradigm, it becomes the role of curriculum theorists and practitioners to propose alternative practices (V), which

---

[4]The trends toward "permissiveness" in child rearing at home and school and which alarmed Bestor were discussed some 15 years later by John W. Aldridge, "In the Country of the Young," a two-part essay in *Harper's Magazine* October/November 1969.

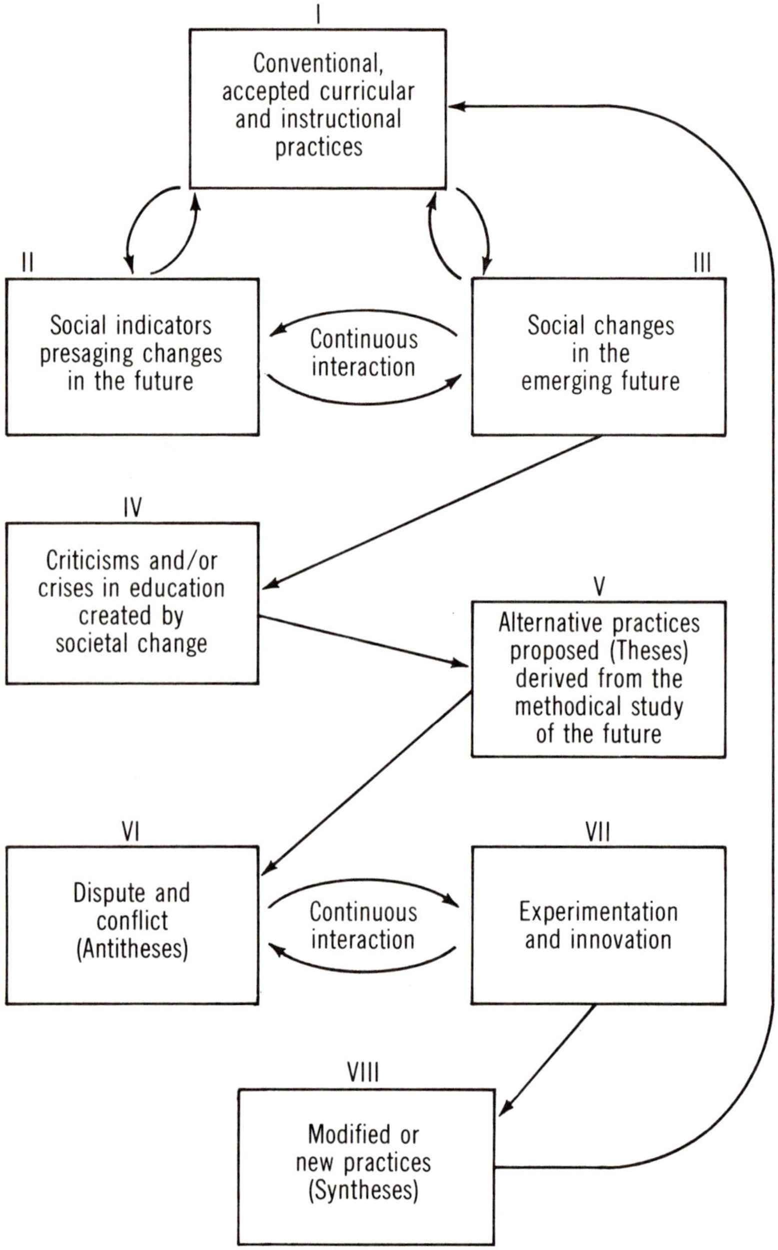

Fig. 5. A paradigm illustrating the structure of evolutionary educational change derived from emerging images of the future

must be defended in subsequent conflict (VI) with their opponents. Eventually, data stemming from experimentation and new ideas (VII) lead to the modification and refinement of new practices (VIII). As consensus is reached as to what societal changes require of education, the new proposals and practices that survive become accepted. Then, as these practices become institutionalized, the cycle begins anew in a manner analogous to Kuhn's scientific revolutions.

Curriculum change: a response to the future. The discarding of outmoded ideas and the introduction of new, promising, instructional practices will inevitably occur if the views expressed by many of the scholars interviewed prove valid. For example, if, as a consequence of diminishing resources, industrial, energy-intensive nations must adapt to using less energy, to recycling resources, and to other forms of conservation, then the educational challenge of the future becomes enormous. In particular, there will be a great need for lifelong learning in order to help persons adapt to a more modest lifestyle.

Planning for Evolutionary Curriculum Change

Curriculum planning to meet the educational needs of the 1990s and beyond seems likely to take two approaches to reform. Advocating the first approach are those teachers and parents who believe that learning experiences should focus on subject matter, on substantive content. The second approach includes those who are proponents of the total development of the learner, those who view the curriculum as the sum of those skills and understandings that the individual, as L. Thomas Hopkins once phrased it, "selects, and incorporates into himself to act with, on, and upon, in subsequent experiences"[5]; namely, a learner-centered approach to education.

The arguments advanced in support of each approach extend back at least to the 19th century. Some of the major arguments for each approach are summarized in the columns below:

Subject-Centered Curriculum	**Learner-Centered Curriculum**
1. Introduces learners to the cultural heritage.	1. Releases the teacher from the pressure to follow a prescribed scope and sequence that does not invariably meet all learners' needs.

[5]L. Thomas Hopkins, *Interaction: The Democratic Process* (Boston: D. C. Heath, 1941), p. 39.

Subject-Centered Curriculum (continued)	**Learner-Centered Curriculum (continued)**
2. Gives the teachers a sense of security by specifying what their responsibilities are for developing given skills and knowledge.	2. Has a positive influence on learners as they find that instruction is varied to meet individual needs and purposes.
3. Reduces repetition or overlap between grade levels or different sections of the same class.	3. Encourages teacher judgment in selecting the content deemed most suitable for a group of learners.
4. Increases the likelihood that learners will be exposed to knowledge and develop skills in an orderly manner.	4. Increases the likelihood that content has relevance to learners.
5. Permits methodical assessment of pupil progress; assumes that knowledge is the only measurable outcome of learning experiences.	5. Modifies instruction to accommodate developmental changes and behavioral tasks as indiviual differences are identified and monitored.
6. Facilitates cooperative group planning by educators in allocating the scope and sequence of learning experiences.	6. Allows much more latitude for creative planning by the individual teacher.

Additional points of disagreement between advocates of the learner-centered and the subject-centered curriculum could be made, but the items above probably suffice to characterize the split in both theory and practice between a traditional or *planned* curriculum and a more open or *planning* approach to curriculum.

An appraisal of alternative curriculum choices. Using our paradigm (fig. 5), how might the practitioner assess the alternative between an emphasis on subject matter or an emphasis on the learner?

Obviously humans need certain survival skills to cope with the coming decades. Also learners need to have an understanding of content in the natural and social sciences and communication skills, including a command of foreign languages. Without such skills and understandings we cannot continue to move toward the humane social consensus to which we are committed in the 20th century:

1. To manage the economy so as to minimize inflation and unemployment.

2. To provide by local, state, or federal government action such services as health care, modest-cost housing, and urban transportation, which are not available to many through the private sector of the economy.

3. To protect the individual from adverse circumstances through such measures as social security, welfare provisions, job safety measures, and control of the disposal of toxic chemical waste.[6]

The need to acquire both substantive skills and humane commitments seems beyond dispute. No reputable educator has ever advocated that the basics be neglected. Nor have educators minimized the importance of developing mature societal insights and social responsibility. The question facing educators is how the curriculum can be structured so as to preserve the merits of a planned, learner-centered approach that encourages social development.

Figure 6, in the form of a cone, depicts the conventional preplanned, subject-centered curriculum. Note that with each passing year the fields of knowledge become increasingly discrete until a distinct compartmentalization becomes visible. Measurable skills and knowledge are emphasized; and the ways in which children learn to do something are given careful consideration. By the middle school years subject matter departmentalization begins to appear; and in high school specific periods exist for the study of mathematics, science, English, and other specialized subjects commonly provided.

Figure 7 represents a curriculum based on a learner-centered approach. Subject matter, a resource stored for use when needed, is represented in the boxes at the right side of the cone. Subject matter feeds into the learning experiences at the heart of the cone. The developmental levels, home backgrounds, and the interests and purposes of young learners, are factors that able teachers take into consideration as they deal with individual differences in students.

In our appraisal of the two models built around pre-selected subject matter and the learners' needs, it seems that both have important virtues when properly implemented by competent, concerned teachers, supervisors, and administrators. We also are convinced that the two models are separated by a chasm, which if it cannot be closed can, at very least, be bridged!

Bridging the gap between the learner-centered and the subject-

---

[6]For a detailed statement on the "social consensus," see John Kenneth Galbraith, "The Conservative Onslaught," *The New York Review of Books*, January 1981, pp. 30-36.

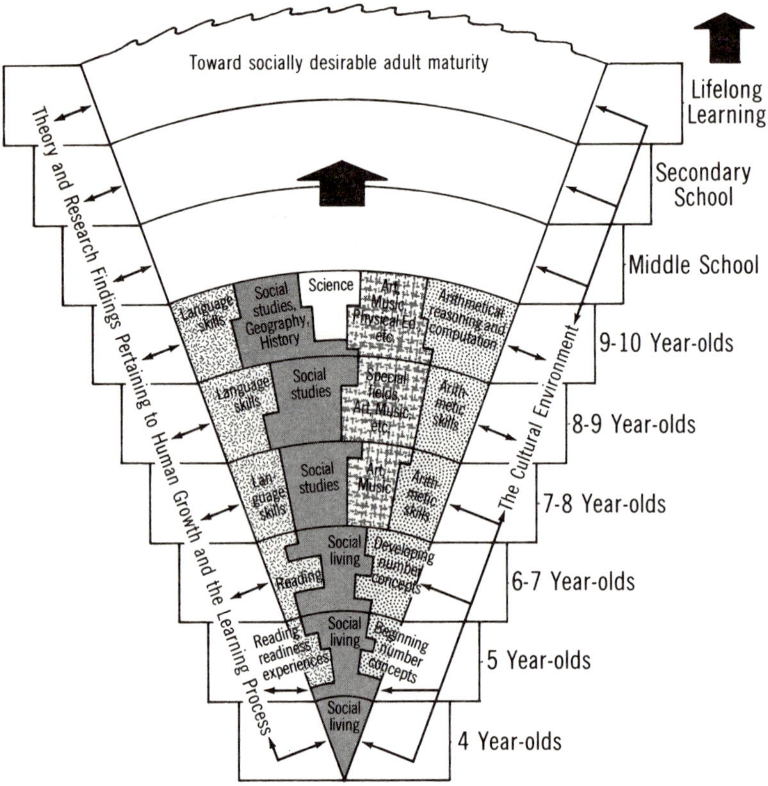

Fig. 6. The pre-planned subject curriculum toward socially desirable adult maturity through mastery of subject content

centered curriculum. To reconcile these two models, we would like to begin with a discussion of the importance of a sense of *security.*

Humans face an insecure future on a troubled globe. As humanistic psychologists long have said, a sense of inner security is necessary if persons are to deal constructively and creatively with their environment. Following this line of thought, it seems prudent to stress learner-centered experiences for the child in the home and in early years of school. A future-focused curriculum presented in figure 7 is one that is free of premature pressure for unreasonable academic per-

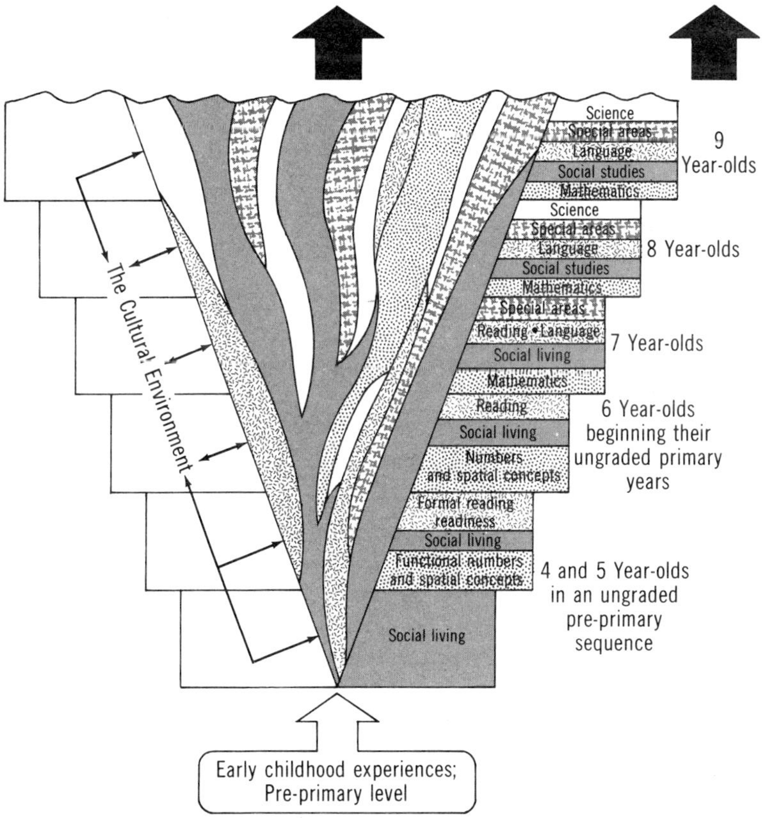

Fig. 7. A learner-centered curriculum based on emergent planning toward socially desirable adult maturity through developmental experiences involving subject matter

formance during the elementary school years and extending into the middle school.

Secure children are those who have grown at their own rate and whose teachers have encouraged them to take as long as they need to develop necessary skills without the stigma of failure. Such children should then be more ready to move with confidence into their advanced years of schooling. In short, we propose a seamless continuum of learning tailored to individual differences, which we shall discuss in greater detail in chapter 8.

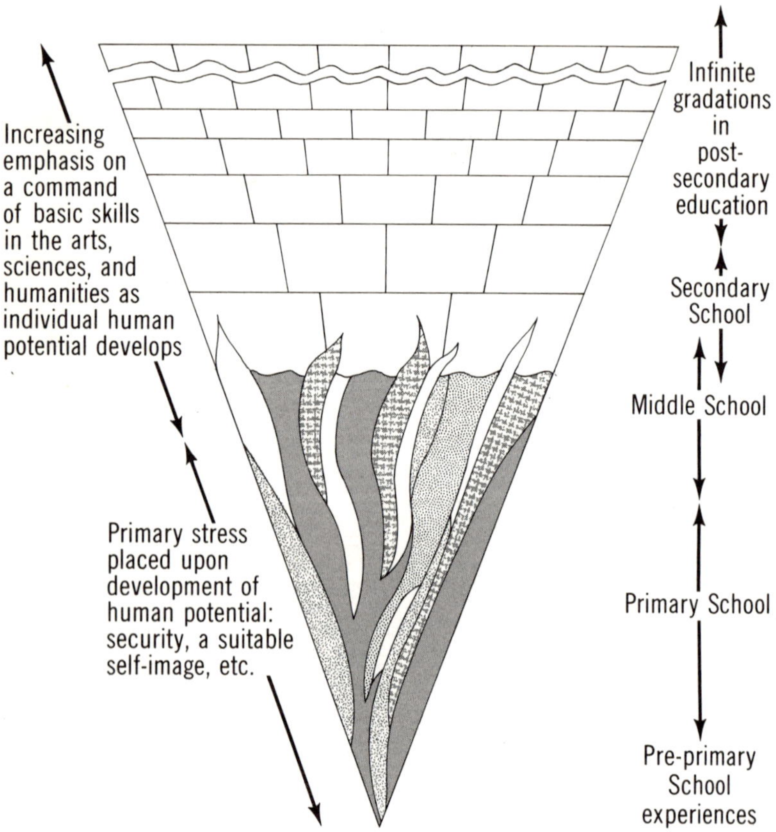

Fig. 8. A composite of the learner-centered and subject centered curriculum

Figure 8, a simplified composite of figures 6 and 7, suggests how a learner-centered curriculum might be phased into one that gradually emphasizes greater concentration on content.

Proposed Guidelines for Curriculum Planning in the Next Two Decades

On the assumption that survival skills and a foundation for good interpersonal relationships can be blended into a future-focused curriculum, let us turn now to the second phase of curriculum development and suggest appropriate guidelines for curriculum change.

Our many hours of discussion with our panel of scholars have resulted in five broad generalizations for an educationally sound, future-oriented curriculum design that involves:

1. introducing learners of all ages to the realities of the world that surrounds them;
2. making clear to learners that to get something of value one must give something of value;
3. understanding that people have various options or alternatives open to them and that each option or alternative has consequences;
4. learning that one must evaluate alternative courses of action and choose wisely among them; and
5. exposing learners to the processes of group action and to cooperative participation in group decision making so that they know how to follow through.

These guidelines are examined in more detail in the next paragraphs.

World realities. In the lifetimes of today's senior citizens much of the world has emerged from an era of economic and often political domination during which global resources were exploited by a few highly industrialized nations. A future-oriented curriculum (including the media which, as Neil Postman points out, have their own curriculum)[7] needs to make clear, in a manner appropriate to students' ages, the nature of todays' global disruptions. This includes the confusion, the uncertainties expressed by the world leaders at the apex of power, the economic transformations, in short, the various emerging concepts which our panel of scholars emphasized.

Giving something of value to obtain something of worth in return. Whether in ecology or economics, political science or sociology, the concept of the trade-off—of giving something valued in return for something one wants—comes through loud and clear. Roy Amara contends that the central issue to be faced by the U.S. is whether our political democracy can cope effectively with the new set of problems demanding long-term perspectives and solutions that will help insure that "our strength of diversity does not become our Achilles' heel of divisiveness. . . ."[8] The good curriculum will need to introduce honorable compromise and respect for others!

Learning to evaluate and to select wisely among options. Here we come to grips with value-based choices that require answers to some basic questions. What is our vision of the good life, and what choices

---

[7]Neil Postman, *Education as a Conserving Activity* (New York: Delacorte Press, 1979), chapters 2-6.

[8]"Roy Amara Looks at the 80's," *Newsletter* (Menlo Park: The Institute for the Future, Summer 1980), p. 3. (Dr. Amara is president of the Institute.)

will help to bring it into being? What is the relationship of alternative choices to the general welfare and to individual welfare? What is the nature of enlightened self-interest?

Exposure to follow-through experiences. Dealing with world realities, trade-offs, and value judgments is meaningless if learners are not introduced to the ways in which group consensus and group action can be implemented. This follow-through, this cooperative social action, is the distinctive characteristic of democracy. But it is not easy to attain!

Learners need to discover how interaction can be made to eventuate in action; how to use time so that making decisions does not degenerate into endless debate; how to avoid the intransigence and divisive tactics of special-interest minorities or single-interest groups; and how to delegate jobs, once a decision is made, so that too many pilots aren't trying to steer the follow-through experiences. Also, it is important to emphasize the point that while the group action supersedes authoritarian dictates, there is nonetheless a need for gifted leaders who provide direction by the merit of their ideas and the authoritativeness of their data.

Theory $\rightleftarrows$ Practice

Theory and practice are intimately related, as the double arrows in the heading above suggest. It is a moot question whether theory precedes practice or whether the experience of practitioners leads to theory. For our purposes we have begun with theories as to how the future, as envisioned by scholars, anticipates a curriculum that offers concepts for successful living for the present and in times to come.

In the next chapter we examine how one can move effectively from concept to curriculum content; namely, the important task of transposing theory into practice!

6

From Concept to Content in the Curriculum

> *Towards what ultimate point is society tending by its industrial progress? When progress ceases, in what condition are we to expect that it will leave mankind?*
>
> —John Stuart Mill

The most interesting and profound concepts are of little practical value to educators unless they can be incorporated into the curriculum. For this reason, we now examine briefly some of the elements involved in curriculum changes that appear to be needed as we move toward the year 2000.

Elements Involved in Curriculum Development

Teachers, curriculum specialists, and administrators draw on a variety of personal and professional experiences as they design the scope and sequence of learning experiences. Some of the elements involved in curriculum development are:

- an educational philosophy that includes an image of the good life, the good society of the future, and a viewpoint toward knowledge and learning that determines which of the two approaches to curriculum theory—subject-centered or learner-centered—will be followed in a given situation;
- certain general goals or objectives that the curriculum is designed to teach;
- assumptions from the fields of human development and learning theory that will guide the instructional practices in the curriculum guide.

These elements provide the "connective tissue" that holds together the educator's conceptions of such things as the relationships between subject matter fields and the structure of knowledge in a substantive field such as geography or physics. They also determine the views that an educator holds with regard to what constitutes the "best" type of school, how learning occurs, how it should be paced, and what policies ought to govern provisions for individual differences, and so on.

Content for a Lifelong Educational Continuum

Figure 9 shows how philosophy, objectives, and ideas regarding human development can be used in planning curriculum content and the scope and sequence of learning experiences.[1] While education and learning are lifelong, for the sake of simplicity this scheme extends only from the early childhood years through the early adolescent period.

At the right side of the cube are developmental levels (I) ranging from nursery school through the upper middle school. At the top of the cube (II) are some of the various social functions and basic activities in which humans engage: recreation, education, aesthetic activities, understanding moral and spiritual values, and the like.

On the front of the cube (III) are various areas around which the school might seek to develop substantive knowledge, in this instance with emphasis on the social studies. We have chosen the social studies for our illustration, because both the natural and social scientists participating in our inquiry reiterated the importance of learners developing historical, anthropological, political, and geographic-demographic understanding of all the world.[2]

At the base of the cube and radiating upward are the broad objectives of education represented by the durable seven Cardinal Principles of Education, probably the most widely quoted statement of objectives in U.S. education:

1. Health
2. Command of fundamental processes
3. Worthy home membership
4. Vocation
5. Civic education
6. Worthy use of leisure
7. Ethical character

Published by the National Education Association in 1918, the Cardinal Principles were the work of a national commission on sec-

---

[1]"Content" as used here and elsewhere has the broadest of connotations. It refers to a lifelong series of learnings, including many that may occur beyond the school walls and at any age.

[2]Specific concepts that might be developed in the social studies, mathematics, and the sciences are elaborated in chapter 8.

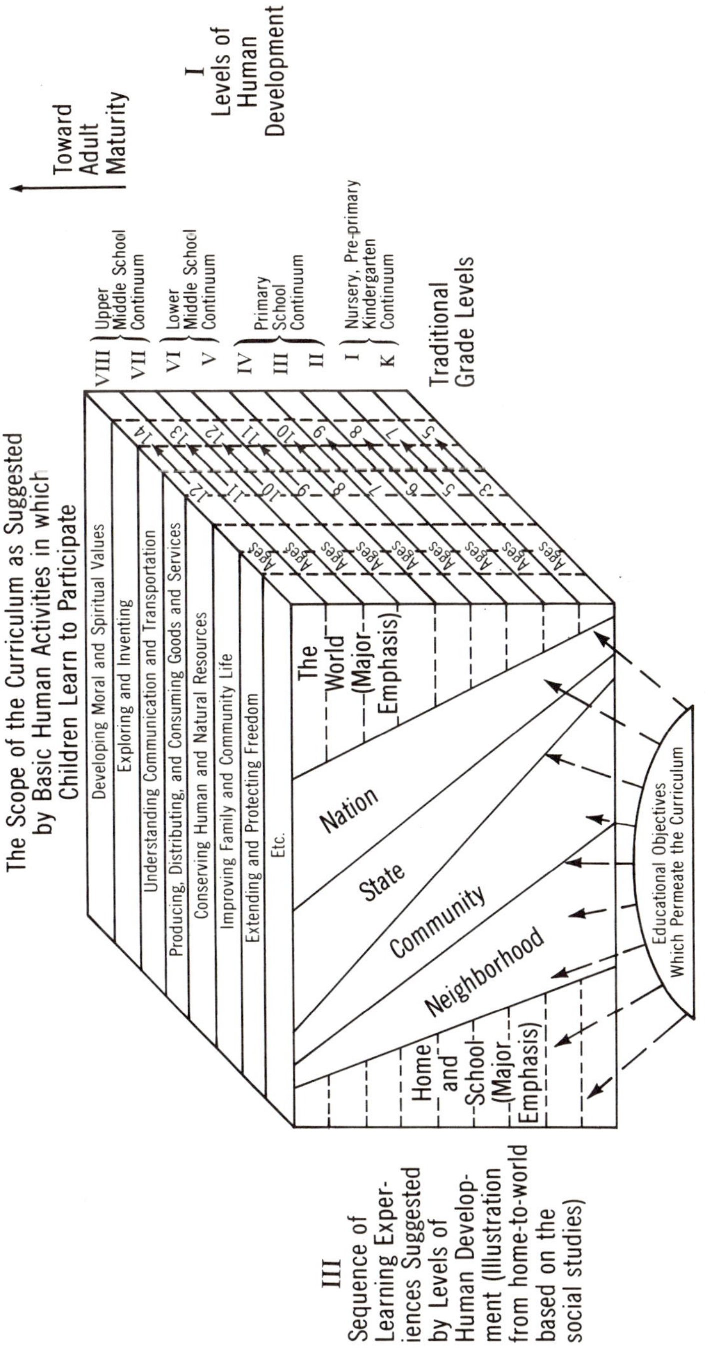

Fig. 9. Elements involved in selecting content for a lifelong educational continuum

ondary education that included such distinguished persons as Thomas H. Briggs, William H. Kilpatrick, and James Hosic. The seven principles have repeatedly been reviewed and their interpretations updated, most recently in 1976.[3]

On the pages that follow, for purposes of comparison, we present excerpts from a statement of goals prepared in 1980 by the Committee on Research and Theory of the Association for Supervision and Curriculum Development (ASCD).[4] The similarity of these 10 objectives to the Cardinal Principles reflect both the prescience of the NEA committee reporting over 60 years ago and the point that modifications in these goals are required by rapid changes in the present era. For instance, "interpreting the world" and "coping with change" are important additions.

Goals of Education

1. Basic Skills

Acquires information and meaning through observing, listening, and reading

Shares information and expresses meaning through speaking, writing, and nonverbal means

Manipulates symbols and uses mathematical reasoning

2. Developing a Self-Concept

Recognizes that self-concept is acquired in interaction with other people

Distinguishes among many concepts of self in various roles or social situations

3. Understanding Others

Bases actions and decisions on the knowledge that individuals differ yet are similar in many ways

Bases actions and decisions on the understanding of lifestyles or behaviors within the context of the value system of the societies in which they were learned

Seeks interactions and feels comfortable with others who are different in race, religion, social level, or personal attributes as well as those who are similar in these characteristics

4. Using Accumulated Knowledge to Interpret the World

Applies basic principles and concepts of the sciences, arts, and humanities to interpret personal experiences

---

[3]See "The Seven Cardinal Principles of Education Revisited," *Today's Education*, September/October 1976, pp. 57-72.

[4]Wilbur R. Brookover et al., *Measuring and Attaining the Goals of Education* (Alexandria, Va.: ASCD, 1980). (The goals listed here are excerpts from a longer, more comprehensive statement.)

Applies basic principles and concepts of the sciences, arts, and humanities to analyze and act upon public issues

Applies basic principles and concepts of the sciences, arts, and humanities to evaluate technological progress

5. Continuous Learning

Bases actions and decisions on the knowledge that it is necessary to continue to learn throughout life because of the inevitability of change

6. Mental and Physical Well-Being

Avoids, to the extent possible, consuming materials harmful to health, particularly addictive ones

Adapts to environmental constraints while seeking to change destructive elements in the environment

Participates in satisfying leisure-time activities

7. Participation in the Economic World of Production and Consumption

Bases decisions on an awareness and knowledge of career options

Makes informed consumer decisions based on appropriate knowledge of products, needs, and resources

8. Responsible Societal Membership

Acts consonant with an understanding of the basic interdependence of the biological and physical resources of the environment

Acts in accordance with a basic ethical framework incorporating those values contributing to group living, such as honesty, fairness, compassion, and integrity

9. Creativity

Entertains and values the imaginative alternatives of others

10. Coping with Change

Entertains new perceptions of the world

Tolerates ambiguity

Acts with an appreciation that, in a changing world, flexibility and adaptability are strengths rather than weaknesses

Selects viable alternatives for actions in changing circumstances

Content Selection, Educational Goals, and Human Development

Everything we teach and everything we hope children will learn is mediated by the developmental levels through which learners pass. This section summarizes some of the work of human developmental specialists whose views have influenced curriculum planning. They include Willard Olson, Erik H. Erikson, Abraham H. Maslow, and Robert J. Havighurst, all of whom have helped teachers during the past 30 years to understand how human development determines the scope and sequence of what is learned.

One of Olson's major contributions is the concept of organismic age, the idea that varying rates of individual growth, both mental and physical, should mediate the curriculum and determine the appropriate instructional method to match individual needs.[5]

Erikson, a psychoanalyst, identified eight stages[6] through which humans pass between birth and maturity. At each stage, as he saw it, there were certain problems to be solved. His views on how humans successfully solve these problems have a bearing on the pursuit of learning throughout life and hence are of value to curriculum planners.

Maslow, a psychologist and well-known psychophilosophical writer, proposed the provocative idea of self-actualization, which he describes as "an episode, or a spurt in which the powers of the person come together in a particularly efficient and intensely enjoyable way."[7] A number of writers in education in the 1960s and 1970s began to see the relevance of his ideas, including his inventory of factors related to psychophysical health, to a good classroom environment.

Of the human development specialists mentioned here, Robert Havighurst is probably the most well-known to U.S. teachers. A sociologist as well as educator, Havighurst proposed the idea of developmental tasks that describe the biosocial and psychological tasks that confront us from birth to old age. Educators need to understand the total context of Havighurst's lifelong developmental tasks as they undertake curriculum development work. These tasks appear below.

Havighurst's Developmental Tasks[8]

Developmental Tasks of Infancy and Early Childhood

Learning to walk
Learning to take solid foods
Learning to talk
Learning to control the elimination of body wastes
Learning sex differences and sexual modesty
Achieving physiological stability

---

[5]Willard Olson, *Child Development* (Boston: D. C. Heath, 1949).

[6]Erik H. Erikson, *Childhood and Society*, 2nd ed. (New York: W. W. Norton 1963).

[7]Abraham H. Maslow, *Toward a Psychology of Being* (New York: Litton Educational Publishing, Inc., 1962), p. 23.

[8]Robert J. Havighurst, *Developmental Tasks and Education* (New York: Longmans, Green, and Company, 1950).

Forming simple concepts of social and physical reality

Learning to relate emotionally to parents, siblings, and other people

Learning to distinguish right and wrong and developing a conscience

Developmental Tasks of Middle Childhood

Learning physical skills necessary for ordinary games

Building wholesome attitudes toward oneself as a growing organism

Learning to get along with age-mates

Learning an appropriate sex role

Developing fundamental skills in reading, writing, and calculating

Developing concepts necessary for everyday living

Developing conscience, morality, and a scale of values

Developing attitudes toward social groups and institutions

Developmental Tasks of Adolescence

Accepting one's physique and accepting a masculine or feminine role

Establishing new relationships with age-mates of both sexes

Achieving emotional independence of parents and other adults

Achieving assurance of economic independence

Selecting and preparing for an occupation

Developing intellectual skills and concepts necessary for civic competence

Desiring and achieving socially responsible behavior

Preparing for marriage and family life

Building conscious values in harmony with a scientific world-picture

Developmental Tasks of Early Adulthood

Selecting a mate

Learning to live with a marriage partner

Starting a family

Rearing children

Managing a home

Getting started in an occupation

Taking on civic responsibility

Developmental Tasks of Middle Age

Achieving adult civic and social responsibility

Establishing and maintaining an acceptable standard of living

Assisting teenage children to become responsible and happy adults

Developmental Tasks of Middle Age (continued)

Developing adult leisure-time activities
Relating to one's spouse as a person
Accepting and adjusting to the physiological changes in middle age
Adjusting to aging parents

Developmental Tasks of Later Maturity

Adjusting to decreasing physical strength and health
Adjusting to retirement and reduced income
Adjusting to death of spouse
Establishing an explicit affiliation with one's age group
Meeting social and civic obligations
Establishing satisfactory physical living arrangements

Using basic human activities for content selection. A second important consideration in curriculum development revolves around basic human activities, some of which are suggested on the top surface of the cube in figure 9.

Using basic human activities as a source of content can be traced back to the 1937 Virginia curriculum study initiated by the Virginia State Superintendent of Public Instruction Sidney B. Hall. Under the direction of Hollis L. Caswell, and with such distinguished consultants as William A. Brownell and Paul R. Hanna, a dedicated staff developed a curriculum guide for grades 1 through 8 that ran to 510 pages! It was built around an extensive list of aims of education and included such items as an "understanding of the interdependence of all forms of life." One of the enduring contributions of the Virginia curriculum study was the idea of building the curriculum around "major functions of social living."[9] These social functions are comparable to the list at the top of the cube which is an abridgement of the more extensive list in the Virginia guide.

The basic human activities shown on the cube are similar to many of the concepts recommended by our panel of scholars; hence, they can be used as guidelines for curriculum change.

Curriculum content and "the coming together of the world." In one context or another, many of our panelists mentioned the concept that Robert F. Byrnes called "the coming together of the world." They also saw this growing interdependence as inevitable. In terms of communication, travel, international relationships, and the use of the

[9]Still relevant after nearly 50 years, the major functions of social living identified by Caswell et al. were: protection and conservation, production and distribution, consumption, communication and transportation, recreation, expression of aesthetic impulses, expression of religious tendencies, education, extension of freedom, integration of the individual, and exploration and invention.

earth's raw materials, the world is becoming ever more interdependent. As a result the world needs, now more than ever, people who can make intellectual and moral sense of the contributions of science and technology.

The third face on our cube presents another aspect of the task of turning concepts into content. This involves moving from understandings of the near-at-hand in the home and school to the "survival and humane living knowledge" that changing times will require. This face of the cube depicts the need for an emerging emphasis on the world with respect to history, geography, and other related disciplines that lend themselves to the fusion of content in the social studies.

Another consideration in presenting subject matter about the world to children are the implications of American-style democracy for the future of a world where justice is denied large groups, ignorance is widespread, and self-interest is more often the rule than the exception. Let us, then, examine the challenging question of how we can help children and youth learn to live with others whose cultures and perspectives on life differ from ours.

Transferring Concept to Content in a Multicultural World

With the increasing interdependence of the world's peoples, it is essential that children and youth learn to understand others and use their accumulated knowledge to interpret the world. One of the first ways in which we can help learners interpret the world is by building cross-cultural insights within our own multi-ethnic nation. With this beginning, our young people can then move out to a world in which there are literally thousands of cultures and subcultures. Some indications of the enormous array of cultures in the world are reflected in the Soviet Union's need to publish textbooks in 53 languages and the fact that more than 200 languages or dialects are spoken in just one African state—Nigeria!

Culture and curriculum content. Understanding other cultural groups—overseas and in our own country—is one of the most important lessons to be extracted from the interviews we conducted with our panel of scholars. Since we are here concerned with making the concept-to-content transition, let us look at what might be done to help our youth avoid the attitude that *my* culture is better than *your* culture. As Leonard S. Kenworthy recognized years ago:

> It is no simple task to introduce boys and girls to this vast, complicated, changing, world community. It cannot be done by adding

> another subject to the already overburdened curriculum; it must be done by having the world dimension added to all phases of existing subjects. It cannot be done by the social studies field alone; it must be done by the work in all fields. It cannot be done by the memorization of isolated facts about the world; it must be done by emphasis upon the information and change of attitudes, the acquisition of skills, and the development of some big concepts.[10]

As one approach to these difficult tasks we propose a culture-centered component that permeates the total life in the school. This suggestion is adapted from the work of one of the panel of scholars, anthropologist Edward T. Hall. In his influential book, *The Silent Language,* Hall describes a "map of culture" developed in cooperation with a colleague, linguist George L. Trager. Noting that Americans are guilty of great ethnocentrism, Hall points out that "we manage to convey the impression that we simply regard [other] nationals as underdeveloped Americans."[11] To remedy our being "in the stone age of human relations in the overseas field," Hall urges that we make an effort to understand 10 basic human activities that exist in a given culture. These he calls Primary Message Systems (PMS). Hall believes that it is necessary for learners of every age to begin to understand that humans see, think, feel, and act the way they do because of the particular subculture in which they have membership.

The ten components of the Primary Message System are:

1. Interaction, including speech and body language
2. Association, including "pecking order"
3. Subsistence, food habits, economic activity
4. Bisexuality, or sex roles
5. Territoriality or status concepts
6. Temporality, i.e., interpretations of time
7. Learning, including variations in how we learn to learn
8. Play, including places and times and various ideas of competition
9. Defense, subsuming psychological and religious mechanisms
10. Exploitation, i.e., use of materials.[12]

A culture-centric curriculum. In figure 10, an application of PMS to education, we suggest how understandings of the PMS might be phased into the curriculum. The first culture to which the learners

---

[10]Leonard S. Kenworth, *Introducing Children to the World* (New York: Harper 1956), p. 201.

[11]Edward T. Hall, *The Silent Language*. 7th ed. (New York: Doubleday-Fawcett Premier Books, 1966), p. 9.

[12]Detailed explanations of each of the ten cultural components in Hall's book are found on pp. 46-62. Also see the Trager-Hall model, pp. 174-175, *The Silent Language*.

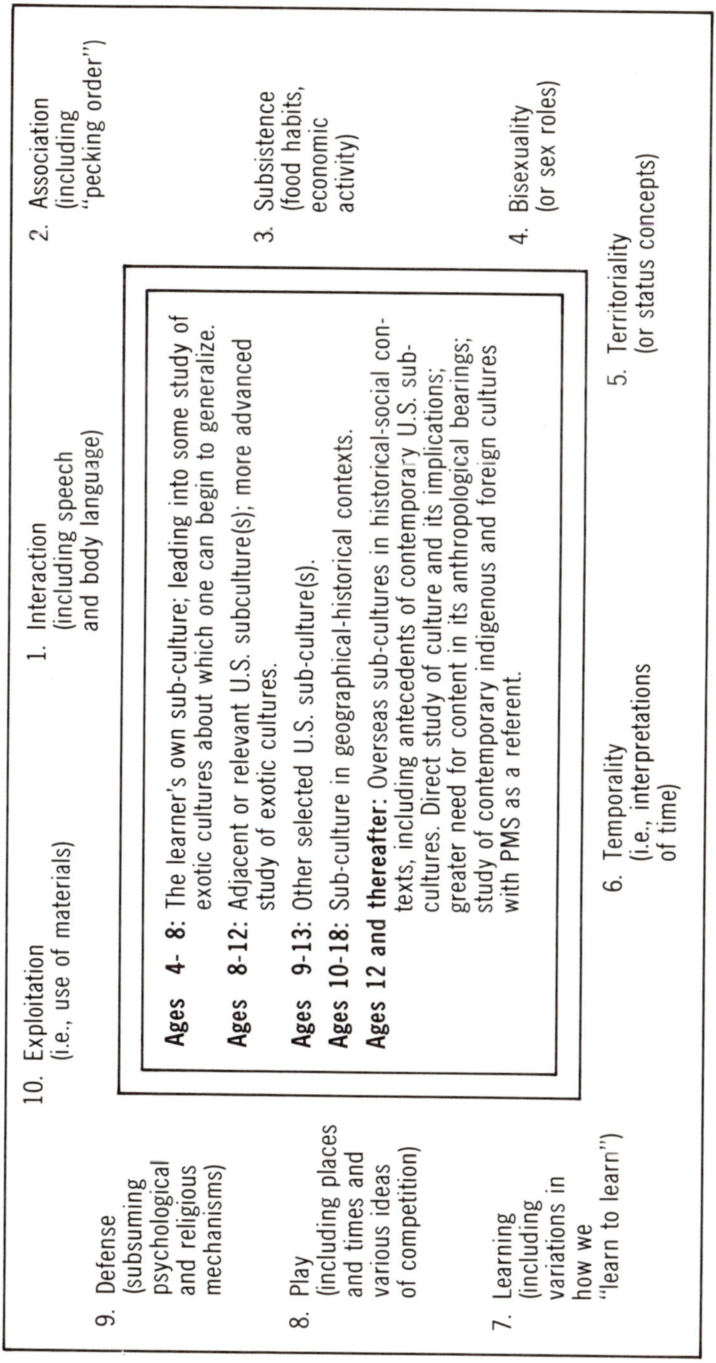

Fig. 10. Primary message systems applied to education

would be exposed is the male/female culture and sex roles in their own home and neighborhood during the four-to-eight-year age range. In the eight-to-twelve-year age span relevant U.S. subcultures would be introduced with the emphasis gradually shifting to study of advanced exotic cultures. We do not, however, mean that a curriculum for a new millennium should revert to yesterday's frequently misleading or stereotyped units about rain forest children on the equator, or Navajos, or nomadic Arabs!

Based on Hall's PMS, it presumably would be suitable for four-to-eight-year-olds to learn about sex roles and occupational roles in their immediate culture and about sources of goods and of food production in their local economy. A year or two later, subcultures such as native Americans and Hispanic Americans might be studied and comparisons made between the subculture and one's own.

Some values of cross-cultural study. Since a culture-centric dimension has rarely been systematically used in curriculum construction, a few concluding comments about such an approach are in order. First, the PMS cultural map developed by Hall and Trager is based on research, hence it provides a source for identifying those basic human activities or social functions that can serve as a basis for curriculum development. Second, it seems logical to approach a study of world cultures after first having introduced young people to their own local and national cultures and subcultures. Third, it seems consistent with the advice of a number of our panel of scholars to begin early to help children understand that human behavior is derived from or influenced by culture. Understanding this concept should help reduce interpersonal friction among the young and enhance mutual trust, good will, and cooperation. Fourth, in a time of rapid change and transformation in U.S. and global lifestyles, cross-cultural and multi-ethnic insights need to be strengthened by seizing opportunities in all areas as well as in nonacademic experiences provided by athletic events, social occasions, and work situations outside the classroom.

Summary

In this chapter we have dealt with the task of turning concepts into curriculum content. We have attempted to show how our image of a good society, educational goals, and factors in individual human development determine the curriculum content. We concluded with some suggestions as to how a multicultural tone might be incorporated into the curriculum by using an adaptation of Hall's Primary

Message Systems. Four guidelines in teaching cross cultural understanding brought the chapter to a close.

In the next chapter we shall emphasize how to educate for a new millennium and deal with ways of deriving curriculum designs for the future. Special attention will be given to communication skills, mathematics, science, and the social studies.

7

The Derived Curriculum

A futures oriented curriculum must give young people general skills for coping with interdisciplinary problems and for handling the integration of knowledge and experience.

—Draper L. Kauffman, Jr.

Humanity's greatest problem has never been the absence of solutions to complex problems. Its greatest problem has been the absence of belief in answers.

—Norman Cousins

As educators turn to the task of modifying curricular and instructional practices for the future, they will have to adapt concepts from the scholarly disciplines for use as curriculum content. They must also, as Kauffman suggests, provide students with opportunities that expose them to the interface between learning and living. The task confronting educators, then, is to modify the curriculum and foster a classroom climate that will project learning into an emerging world of continual change with perplexing new problems, but also with many new opportunities.

In chapter 6 we suggested some ways in which the concepts of the scholars might be woven into the curricular and instructional practices for the school of the future. We begin this chapter with a description of the "derived curriculum" that includes real world experiences.

The Derived Curriculum

Our panel of scholars provided some of the raw material needed for curriculum planning. Curriculum workers can use a number of their suggestions to derive programs based on probable futures. However, as Tennyson and Park point out in their study of the teaching of concepts, ". . . the pedagogical structure of knowledge and the optimal structure for learning may be quite different from the forms we find among subject matter experts."[1] Hence our concepts from the scholarly disciplines need to be translated with care to insure their teachability.

Viewpoints on curriculum planning for the year 2000 are found in several sources. Botkin, Elmandjra, and Malitza discussed the idea of "anticipatory" learning—learning which anticipates tomorrow.[2] The idea is also mentioned by panelist Eleanora Masini who made the point that:

> Students can no longer afford the luxury of . . . "disconnected thinking." They should acquire knowledge of the past and present if they are to be a part of "anticipatory education." There is a need for vision which leads to anticipatory thinking and the consideration of alternative solutions. Youngsters must learn that each act must be evaluated in terms of its future impact.
>
> —*Eleanora Masini*

Other relevant comments made by King and Peccei were:

> . . . concepts which I think are important for our youth to acquire include the cultivation of a long-term perspective, adaptability to rapid change and the ability to integrate the many trends in our society and economy; in short, to develop a dynamic and holistic attitude.
>
> —*Alexander King*

> The future is not going just to happen, but is going to be the result of what more than four billion people do daily. Students must learn to act responsibly and purposefully so as to build a better future for them and their children.
>
> —*Aurelio Peccei*

Some of the merits of an anticipatory approach to learning are: 1) it gives students the skills to deal with the future; 2) it helps students to foresee the influence of probable future events; 3) it suggests alternative paths to follow; and 4) it requires that people evaluate the consequences of the alternatives and of the likely trade-offs needed as a result of future decisions.

As we use the term, anticipatory learning is the basis for a curriculum derived from the ongoing review of scholars' concepts of tomorrow. Such approach to the curriculum, we contend, will help educators plan specific goals and classroom practices. In the second part of

---

[1]Robert D. Tennyson and Ok-Choon Park, "The Teaching of Concepts: A Review of Instructional Design Research Literature," *Review of Educational Research*, Spring 1980, p. 55.

[2]James Botkin, Mahdi Elmandjra, and Mircea Malitza, *No Limits to Learning: Bridging the Human Gap* (New York: Pergamon Press, 1979).

this chapter, "Curriculum Content and Classroom Climate," we shall suggest certain goals of the mathematics, science, and social studies curriculum that could be derived from scholars' concepts.

Incorporating Real World Experiences

In addition to deriving a curriculum that incorporates scholars' concepts of the future, we suggest that educators should improve the quality of teaching by extending learning into the real world with its present and future problems. A future-oriented curriculum cannot be implemented effectively if teachers continue to use teaching practices that do not involve genuine student participation in society's problems and processes.

The idea of incorporating real world experiences into the curriculum is hardly a new one to educators. It has been treated in various publications ranging from Paul Hanna's *Youth Serves the Community* (1936) to the "Walkabout" concept,[3] both of which are described in some detail in Appendix A. The notion of participating in action and service learning involving real world experiences must become an integral part of schooling in the future.

Many of our panelists repeatedly voiced support for the idea of real world experiences. George A. Parks of Stanford University, for instance, said that direct experience was the only thing that really helps one learn how to solve problems. On a different continent, a panelist at the University of Glasgow stated emphatically:

> We need to stop thinking of schooling as a preparation for life. It is necessary for students to get out and participate in society and then come back to the school to evaluate. We must get young people to accept an apprenticeship in the affairs of society so that they can get inside what's going on and be involved in the perpetual struggle to improve society.
>
> —*Eric Wilkerson*

In the remainder of this chapter we will present an educational model that combines the idea of a derived curriculum and real world experiences.

Since it is impossible to anticipate the future precisely, the best we can hope to do is to provide youth with certain general skills that should be useful for dealing with change. Carefully selected beyond-the-classroom experiences can help to provide the motivation to

---

[3]Maurice Gibbons, "Walkabout: Searching for the Right Passage from Childhood and Schools," *Phi Delta Kappan*, May 1974, pp. 596-602.

master these skills. In the past, some school systems, particularly at the secondary school level, have incorporated off-campus, firsthand learning in their programs. The writers believe that comparable, direct experiences can be more widely incorporated into the elementary and middle school curriculum as well.

Figure 11 suggests how the components of a derived curriculum and real world experiences can be interlaced to prepare students for lifelong learning. Both the cognitive and affective modes of learning are considered in this model. The cognitive concepts are associated with precepts that teachers can use in selecting suitable learning experiences. The precepts function as guidelines to help teachers build socially desirable skills and insights. The model also suggests how certain practices endow the curriculum with meaning, which, in turn, strengthen the precepts.

Another significant aspect of firsthand, real world experiences is the potential it has for instilling the habit of continuous or lifelong learning by putting students in situations in which they must work out solutions to real life problems. Such experiences remove the barriers between school and life.

Figure 11 also illustrates how input from scholars concerning their ideas of the future can be compiled into an inventory. These concepts can then be restructured by curriculum specialists using sound pedagogical practices to develop the scope and sequence of basic skills that students need to master.

While we are dealing with cognitive content here, it is also important that the learner not be neglected. The personality and interests of students should be assessed, along with community and school resources, to determine the type of real world experiences that can be planned to fit the precepts suggested for the cognitive domain.

The synergistic, and often serendipitous, input from real world learning experiences contribute to personal development both in the school and in the broader environment of the community. Once this habit of learning how to learn is established, it should permeate all phases of students' lives and continue when formal schooling ends. Most future-oriented individuals probably would agree with the following overall goals for education suggested in *No Limits to Learning* cited earlier: 1) identifying future problems, 2) recognizing alternative solutions, 3) analyzing the merits of various alternatives, and 4) making decisions. But these goals cannot be accomplished without a reasonable command of basic tools of communication and mathematics. Unfortunately, the focus in many schools too often has stopped with the basics. The mastery of concepts from our inventory cannot be achieved merely by developing proficiency in speaking,

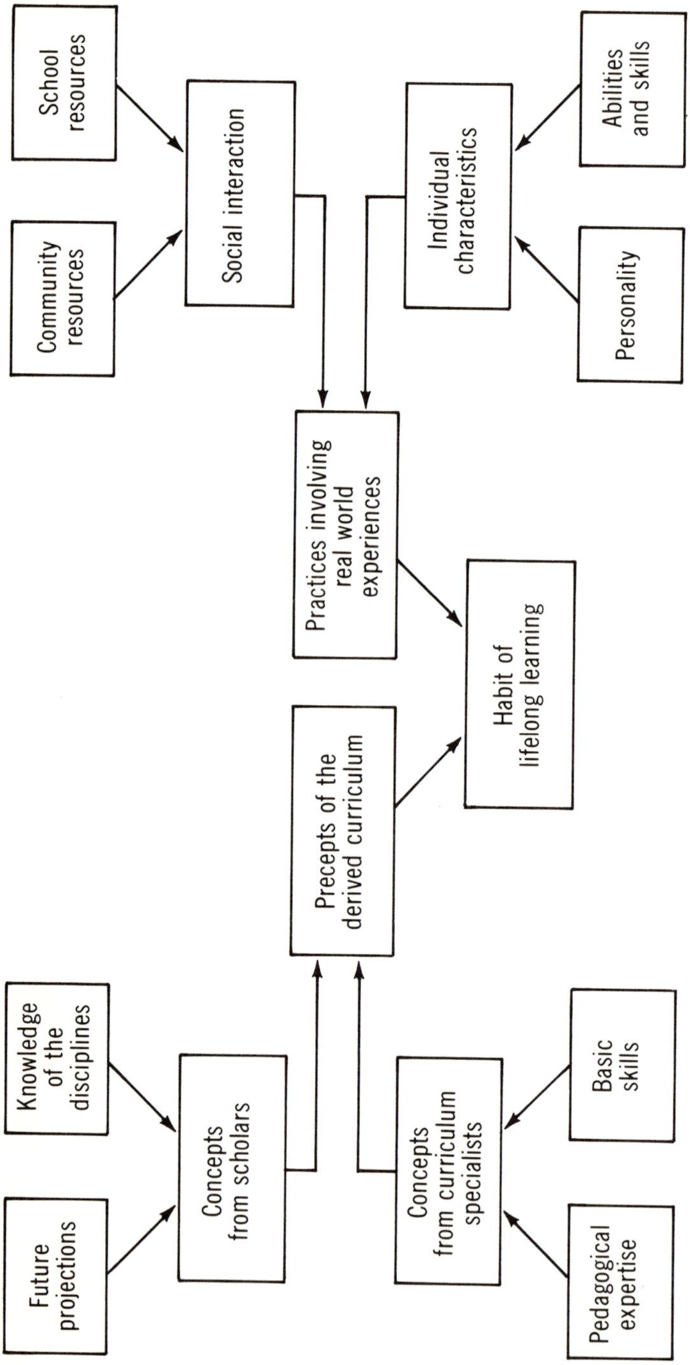

Fig. 11. Coordinated variables in planning a curriculum for lifelong learning

writing, and computing. Life in the future will be far too complex, as our panel of scholars suggest, to consider the present generation educated when they have achieved only these minimal skills.

As our goals for the derived curriculum illustrate, the concept of basic skills is dynamic and emergent, not static. The basic competencies necessary for today are not the same as they were a mere 10 or 20 years ago, nor will today's competencies be exactly the same 10 or 20 years hence. However, they will, at any given time, continue to be rooted in the needs of society, both present and future. For example, the skills involved in basic computation, while still important, are being augmented now by the need for skills in using calculators and computers, skills that will be dealt with more fully later in this chapter.

Throughout our interviews the project staff was impressed by the way many scholars in the natural and social sciences mentioned the importance of verbal communication skills in conjunction with the significant, future survival concepts from within their respective disciplines. Lawrence Wylie of Harvard, for example, suggested that teachers help students understand that social communication depends, to a larger degree than many persons realize, on nonverbal communication. Nonverbal communication will differ from culture to culture, says Wylie; but as more and more cross-cultural contacts occur, effective communication will require a broadened, transethnic view of language. Transethnic communication was a concept considered crucial to tomorrow's world by our panel of scholars, especially the anthropologists cited in chapter 4, who felt that American students needed to broaden their fluency in second languages in order to develop a greater empathy with people of other cultures.

To conclude this section, we reiterate that skills in the three Rs remain basic; but it is imperative that those who are responsible for skills development keep in mind that if learners are to cope with the future, our sights for education must be set higher than competency in the three Rs. As Longfellow wrote more than a century ago, "If you would hit the mark, you must aim above it. Every arrow that flies feels the attraction of earth."

Values and Human Relations

As cultures collide, two areas that curriclum workers should not ignore are ethical values and good interpersonal and intergroup relations. Both of these elements were alluded to in a large number of our interviews. They arose in various contexts such as: 1) the differences between facts and values; 2) values as a necessary reference point for decision making; 3) an ability to understand the forces that bind one's own values and those of another culture or subculture, 4) teacher awareness of the values of the hidden curriculum reflected in their instructional practices; 5) frequent reexamination of values that are changing; and 6) recognition of the need for a transition from material values to a greater respect for human values.

Through experiences beyond the campus, students, with appropriate guidance from their teachers and counselors, will have opportunities on many occasions to examine their own values and become more aware of the values of others. Also, direct contacts with the spectrum of humanity found in most communities should provide students with broadening experiences in appreciating and getting along with elements of society that are different from their own.

Curriculum Content and Classroom Practice

This part of chapter 7 endeavors to show how a future-focused curriculum and real world experiences can improve elementary and middle school mathematics, science, and social studies programs. We have selected these areas of the curriculum because they coincide with the content areas of the scholars from the natural and social sciences on our panel.

Using the concepts gleaned from our interviews and concepts related to the nature of learning, we first propose a list of general goals for mathematics, science, and social studies curriculum. Then we shall select one or two of the goals of a future-derived curriculum and describe some easily implemented, real world experiences that are appropriate for young learners.

The Mathematics Curriculum in a Microtechnological Age

Mathematics concepts from the scholars. Several concepts germane to the mathematics curriculum of the future can be found in our inventory. They are summarized in the following statements:

- With the extraordinary strides made in the area of microtechnology in the 1970s and the promise of more advances in the 1980s, we in the industrialized nations are living in a technocentric age.
- The citizens of tomorrow must learn to cope with the growing influence of computerization of the "Robot Revolution"[4] and be able to use it appropriately in the information economy that is already well-established.
- Cybernetics has the potential for becoming an invaluable aid in achieving many social, scientific, and industrial goals.

---

[4]See "The Robot Revolution," *Time*, 8 December 1980, pp. 72-83.

• The study of artificial intelligence via computers promises to increase human reasoning powers and our understanding of the ability to reason.

• The heuristics of problem solving rooted in a command of basic skills should become the main focus of mathematical education in the future.

• Original ideas, explorations, and divergent thinking should be encouraged in mathematical contexts.

Goals of a future-focused mathematics curriculum. Using these concepts, it becomes possible to derive three goals which might appear in the mathematics curriculum of the future.

1. All students should be conversant with the role and the impact of computers in society and become aware of both their limitations and potential.
2. Each student should understand what computers are and know when and how to use them.
3. Problem solving and other nontechnological (humanistic, intuitive, creative) skills also should be emphasized in mathematics.

These goals require a bit of explanation. In the 1970s and early 1980s many mathematics educators began to urge greater use of calculators, beginning at the elementary level. They also urged modifications in evaluation instruments to make them relevant with respect to calculator programs. Rapid advances in microtechnology make the need for a "computer-conscious curricula" even more urgent. As computers invade many more aspects of everyday life, students cannot be sheltered from them because of occasional protests that they threaten to dilute the mastery of basic skills.

Failure to introduce and to use calculators and computers in school creates a needless barrier between what is happening in students' everyday lives and what they are being taught in school. Furthermore, now that the computer is so ubiquitous outside of school, computer literacy will become a basic skill for the new millennium. We must not be argued into conceiving basic mathematics skills to be the same as they were in the dawning age of the computer back in the 1950s and 1960s. For mathematics education to remain viable in the future, it must include a major role for the computer now.

The first two goals of our future-derived mathematics curriculum are related to computer literacy; the third goal for mathematics classrooms should be the creation of environments for problem solving that can be directly tied into the first two goals.

While several scholars mentioned that computers would reduce much of the mechanical work necessary in our society, they pointed out that we need also to stress uniquely human skills in our schools. Problem solving with its fundamental components of active exploration, creativity, heuristics, and intelligent guessing cannot be delegated to computers. Problem solving should be the focus of instruction in mathematics, and the computer can facilitate the problem solving.

To sum up, there are two ingredients that should influence the tone of teaching mathematics in the future. The first is a climate where genuine problem solving flourishes; the second is an emphasis on the heuristics of problem solving. This will require a substantial departure from traditional routines, recipes, and formulas, and their replacement with unique, individual approaches that are the creation of each student.

Real world mathematics in a computerized society. Many of the real world experiences related to computers can take place within the school system. A number of school districts now have computer facilities for secondary students, and more elementary schools are acquiring them each year. Where computer facilities are available, plans should be made to wire schools into the main computer. In the interim, the elementary and middle school can invest in the present generation of inexpensive microcomputers.

Instruction in the use of computers should begin at the awareness level for elementary school children and continue through the rest of their schooling in mathematics. While students will acquire these skills at a different pace and at varying levels of sophistication, here are a few general suggestions for intelligent use of computer technology with elementary and middle school students. Bear in mind that the precepts and practices listed are merely a few examples of what might be done. They are not intended to be viewed as a course of study.

Elementary School Level

Precept

Computers serve us in many ways.

Practice

Investigate and record all the ways computers are used in your community. Examine home uses. Bring in examples of computer bills. Visit a computer center, a bank, a hospital, or a library to see how computers are used.

Precept

Computers are machines; there are many kinds of computers.

Practice

Examine computer hardware: microprocessors, tapes, punch cards, CRT and printing machines, terminal keyboard.

Precept

Computers get their information from humans.

Practice

Examine the ways computers are given information. Make punch cards that describe the characteristics of your family, class, school, and community.

Precept

Computers can be used to play games.

Practice

Introduce the computer and develop logic and strategic thinking skills by playing games on a preprogramed computer.

Precept

There are many computer occupations.

Practice

Visit a computing center. Describe the jobs that different employees perform.

Precept

Computers can help you learn in reading, math, social studies, and other subjects.

Practice

Complete an appropriate computer-assisted instruction (CAI) skill program in the various subject areas.

Middle School Level

Precept

A flow chart is a map to the precise, logical ordering of what you want the computer to do.

Practice

Write a flow chart for: waking up and going to school in the morning; doing a multiplication problem.

Precept

Computers use different languages.

Practice

Introduce BASIC or another simple computer language.

Precept

A program translates a flow chart into computer language.

Practice

Use your multiplication flow chart to write a program and run it through a computer.

Precept

Computers can help solve problems.

Practice

Write a computer program to solve problems from your mathematics text.

Precept

Computers can simulate situations that allow you to see the outcomes of different decisions.

Practice

Present situations with different possible outcomes (desirable and undesirable) by manipulating variables.

The Science Curriculum in a Resource-Depleted Environment

Science concepts from the scholars. A 1980 report commissioned by the White House concluded that many Americans could become scientific illiterates if the quality of science programs in our schools continues its current decline.[5] The scientists whom we interviewed listed several concepts that will contribute to students' and adults' scientific literacy. They can be summarized as follows:

- The citizens of tomorrow must understand the basic principles of science and laws of nature in order to deal with the science they encounter in their everyday lives.
- Students must learn to make science-related choices and decisions on a rational basis.
- The interdependence of the elements in our environment should lead to an appreciation of ecological holism.
- Students must understand the generation, depletion, and limitations of world energy resources.
- Science and all that it encompasses, including life itself, is in a constant state of flux and creation.

These concepts, presented at greater length in chapters 3 and 4, need to be incorporated in science curricula for the future. The fact that our panel of scholars from different fields of expertise mentioned

---

[5]"U.S. Report Fears Most Americans Will Become Scientific Illiterates," *The New York Times*, 23 October 1980, p. A22.

science-related concepts is convincing evidence that science and technology are influencing almost every aspect of our lives. How, then, might we begin to improve the science experiences of children and youth?

Goals for a future-oriented science curriculum. The writers offer the following general goals as a partial answer for a future-oriented science curriculum:

1. Students should understand the omnipresent role of science and technology in their everyday lives and make ecologically appropriate use of the marvels at their command.

2. Students should, at a suitable time in their development, demonstrate the ability to apply the scientific method of rational thinking to practical, everyday problems.

3. Students should understand the limits of our resources, the consequences of their unrestrained use, and the complicating and potentially dangerous increase in the world population.

4. Students should have experiences using the processes employed by scientists.

In a derived science curriculum, three issues need to be considered: content vs. process approaches to instruction; expository vs. inquiry methods of instruction; and the social context of scientific decision-making. Each of these issues has a direct bearing on the development of the future science curriculum.

Content vs. process. The question of whether educators had overemphasized process at the expense of content in teaching came up repeatedly after the Soviet Union surprised the world by lofting Sputnik. At the time, widespread dissatisfaction was voiced about the science program in American schools. The rationale for emphasizing factual knowledge and mastery of content is clear; namely, in the future young and old alike will need to acquire as much factual information as possible about their environment before they can preserve life and attain decent standards of living on our small planet.

The process approach to learning stresses the teaching of the methods employed by scientists to gain more knowledge. Those who support this point of view argue that facts change as scientists investigate the phenomena of the universe. Students, therefore, should learn how to question dubious facts rather than simply to memorize them. As a case in point, process-learning advocates point out that the flight of Voyager I proved many assumptions and much previous knowledge about the planet Saturn to be incorrect. Many "facts," previously believed to be accurate, have been replaced by new concepts. As future exploration provides even better data, we should be prepared to modify what we earlier considered to be "facts." The basic process approach includes techniques of: 1) observation, 2) inference, 3) prediction, and 4) communication. More complex processes involve the coordination or integration of these four techniques. Some of the higher level processes are: 1) controlling variables, 2) hypothesizing, and 3) experimenting.

From the remarks of the experts involved in our study, it seems reasonable to infer that the most effective approach to teaching science combines both types of learning experiences, but with a somewhat greater emphasis on the process approach. Knowledge of content is important because predicting, hypothesizing, and inferring cannot be done without knowledge of certain facts.

Expository and inquiry teaching. Expository teaching is essentially providing the student with information. Inquiry teaching is setting up situations in which students can explore ideas and discover information independently. Inquiry teaching is thought to give students a more vivid, lasting impression of what they learn. Rather than being told what the facts are or how something is done, students should be allowed, to the extent that school resources and time constraints permit, to experiment and "discover" science for themselves. A key point to remember here is that direct, real world experiences often can provide firsthand scientific information and, in the process, establish habits of inquiry into everyday living and decision making that can last a lifetime. Especially in a world of increasingly rapid scientific discoveries and changes, such inquiry skills are likely to take on greater importance.

The social context. The third issue to consider about the derived science curriculum is that science cannot be taught in isolation from other disciplines. Humans must realize that many of the problems that challenge the sciences cut across a wide variety of subject matter areas. A multi-disciplinary approach is, therefore, highly desirable in solving the complex problems of our planet. The world today is beset with problems that cannot be resolved entirely in the scientific domain. Such problems as resource depletion or pollution require not only scientific solutions; they frequently require knowledge in the sociological, psychological, economic, ethical, and political arenas of contemporary society.

Several of the panelists referred to the troubling circumstances associated with some scientific achievements. For instance, microbiologist Gary Sojka pointed out that such developments as a technology for creating new life-forms, *in vitro* pregnancies, and cloning present legal, moral, and ethical issues with which we are not prepared to cope.

By designing small-scale experiments or by simulations our

schools can begin to evaluate the future impact of technology on society and assess the economic, political, ethical, and legal ramifications involved. The ultimate goal for learners, old and young, is to prepare them to ask the question: What scientific advances can help improve everyone's quality of life now or in the future? In answering this question, decisions can be made, for example, to invest in some ventures such as the space shuttle or to abort others such as the supersonic passenger planes of the U.S. Concorde type.

Science experiences related to energy and the ecosystem. As illustrative of a future-oriented science curriculum, we have chosen the goal of understanding the limitations of our natural resources and the probable consequences if their unrestrained exploitation is continued, a concern voiced by many of our panelists. Since our daily news is dominated by this complex issue and since it directly affects our personal lives, it offers rich opportunities for involving students in real world experiences.[6]

Elementary Levels

Precept

There are many sources of energy around us and some of them are used in virtually every aspect of our daily lives.

Practice

Find out what our main sources of energy are by taking an energy tour of your home, school, and community. Note who uses various forms of energy and what they use it for.

Precept

Many community workers depend on a continuous supply of energy, or they make decisions about energy that affect all of us.

Practice

Examine firsthand, with due regard for the appropriate developmental level of your students, the relationship each of the following has to the uses made of energy: farmer, grocer, barber, oil man, electrician, telephone man, truck driver, meter reader, gas station attendant, mayor, and the city council.

Precept

There are many ways to save or to conserve energy.

Practice

Decide what can be done to conserve energy at school and in the

---

[6]A number of the practices listed here were suggested in publications from the U.S. Department of Energy.

community. Make a list of what you can do at home to conserve energy. Keep a daily checklist of what you actually did to conserve it.

Precept

Transportation requires energy and affects our environment.

Practice

Investigate the amount of energy used and the types of pollution caused by transportation vehicles. Project what the future of transportation might be.

Middle School Level

Precept

Conservation is necessary since resources are dwindling and financial and environmental costs of developing new resources are enormous.

Practice

Check your home, school, other buildings for energy wastage. Test and compare insulation materials by building a small icebox. How can we encourage people to conserve energy?

Precept

Our most highly used form of energy, electricity, comes from many sources.

Practice

List the problems and benefits of each source of electrical power. Which source(s) can and should we use to produce electricity?

Precept

Coal and oil are not only used to produce energy, they are used to manufacture many products from fertilizers to plastics.

Practice

List and discuss the many petroleum and coal products we use. What are some of the most important uses of petroleum? What products in home or school are made from fossil fuels?

Precept

The sun is the most inexhaustible and cleanest source of known energy, but there are many problems associated with solar energy.

Practice

Experiment with different materials to collect solar energy. Should we spend more money for solar energy research?

Precept

Society depends on energy to link people, goods, and services.

Practice

Map the pattern of linkage in your community from the power plant to you. What might happen if this energy network broke down for an hour? A day? A week?

Teaching the Social Studies in a Global Perspective

Social science concepts from the scholars. The interdependence of all persons on the planet led many of the natural and social scientists on our panel to suggest the following concepts as necessary for tomorrow's citizens:

- In our shrinking world all people need to be conversant with world history and its lessons and learn to cope with cultural diversity by communicating with many different cultures.
- The notions of human dignity and equality of opportunity must be recognized as an entitlement for all world citizens.
- Global issues, imbalances, and inequities need to be resolved through necessary trade-offs and enlightened, honorable compromise.
- To understand human behavior we all must keep in mind people's cultural backgrounds and their local problems.
- Both interdisciplinary and planetary perspectives are needed to overcome ethnocentrism and cultural snobbery.

Our derived curriclum for the social studies seeks to tie together political, social, and economic issues in order to understand conflicting national and international interests. This complex entanglement of problems was introduced in chapter 1.

Concepts for a future-derived social studies curriculum.

1. Social justice is the cornerstone of any viable society.
2. Learning about the people of another country can help us understand and appreciate different cultures.
3. The social and economic choices we make always involve trade-offs, i.e., giving something of value in return for something one prizes and seeks.
4. Social institutions and programs designed to improve human welfare have both great potential and certain limitations.
5. Students need to understand the relationship of the governed to the government and of the government to the governed, including fiscal responsibility.

The social studies have the overall goal of teaching the rights and the responsibilities of world citizenry. This came through clearly in our interviews with scientists. Through participation in home, neighborhood, school, community, national, and international activities, on a sequential basis, children and youth gradually can be made aware of the operation, issues, and some of the internal politics of the hierarchical system in which they have membership. As they see how society is run and how changes occur, they also can learn some of the ways in which to modify and to improve the system in a fair, orderly way. One of the problems in many current social studies curricula is that they do not reflect the growing importance of the so-called Third World or developing countries. Social studies in the U.S., as Mehlinger points out, continues to be dominated by American history, with global history and issues treated in a far too cursory a fashion.[7]

Another necessity in a shrinking world of global interdependence will be skill in the art of group decision making. The same skills and insights required for global decisions can also be practiced at the elementary and secondary school levels. Such elements of decision making as mutual support and awareness of long-range consequences are concepts that the schools can foster.[8]

Developing a sense of community on a global scale also seems a highly desirable goal, especially in view of changing family structures in the U.S. In 1980 one out of every three marriages failed; and in one-third of our homes with children of five or younger, a working mother left them to the care and guidance of others. Projections suggest that by the end of this century the number of single and two-person families will increase dramatically. The trend toward disintegration of the traditional nuclear family, coupled with the increasing family mobility reflected in the 1980 census, are two compelling reasons for increasing our efforts to stitch together a greater sense of community, of belonging, for young and old alike.

Real world social studies experiences. This last section presents some examples of experiences that cut across various disciplines of the social sciences: anthropology, sociology, political science, history, and economics. Firsthand, beyond-school-walls learnings continue to receive emphasis.

---

[7]Howard Mehlinger, "Social Studies: Some Gulfs and Priorities" in Howard Mehlinger and O. L. Davis, eds. *1981 Yearbook of the National Society for the Study of Education* (Chicago: University of Chicago Press, 1981).

[8]As widely reported in April of 1981, today's college students appear to be badly informed about the world beyond U.S. shores—a situation which challenges many of our educational policies. In a nationwide survey conducted by the Educational Testing Service, scores ranged from 41.9 as an average score for freshman to 50.5 for seniors on a 101-item quiz on world affairs. Education majors did least well; history or math majors fared best. See "Collegians Get 'F' on World Affairs," *U.S. News and World Report*, 27 April 1981, p. 11.

Elementary Level

Precept

Every choice involves some cost.

Practice

Review some of the choices that the children and their parents have made recently. How and why were they made? What were the advantages and disadvantages of their choices?

Precept

Resources are limited while our wants are unlimited, hence choices must be made.

Practice

Role play, using teacher-made description cards or newspaper clippings that describe individuals with equal and unequal opportunities and results. After the simulation is carried out, describe and discuss some of the feelings each person had. What are some of the advantages and disadvantages of equal opportunities?

Precept

Government in a democracy is influenced by the views and values of a spectrum of diverse people. The government must make decisions that will enhance the well-being of the less fortunate as well as the more fortunate of its citizens.

Practice

Where does the government get its power and money? How does it help you? How does it help some of the people you know? List some of the government services or facilities that you or others use from the federal, state, and local governmental agencies. Do you think cuts should be made in any of these services in order to reduce taxes? Should some services be expanded? Which ones and why?

Middle School Level

Precept

TINSTAAFL (There is no such thing as a free lunch.)

Practice

Make a list of some of the things provided by governmental agencies that appear to be free. Are any really free? In view of your conclusions, what is the true cost of each service, and who pays for it?

Precept

"Free enterprise" is the term generally used to describe our economic system.

Practice

Interview people who have different jobs. Find out how they feel about their work. How do they feel about the free enterprise system? What countries do not have a free enterprise system? What are the advantages and disadvantages of different economic systems?

Precept

People in many countries suffer extreme economic hardship. People in industrialized countries use much more of the world's resources.

Practice

Find out which countries are industrialized and which are less developed. What are some of the problems of each? Some people suggest that the wealth of the world should be redistributed so that everyone has equal access to the world's wealth. What are the advantages and disadvantages of such a plan? If there are children in your school who have arrived recently from another country, spend some time with them so that you can find out what they say life is like in another part of the world.

Summary

In this chapter we have discussed how we believe curriculum content for the future should be influenced by the concepts that natural and social scientists believe people of every age must understand. We also have presented a sampling of these concepts to develop the idea of a "derived curriculum," one based on projected images of the future and the skills needed to cope with that future. We have also stressed that firsthand or real world experiences are necessary if the curriculum is to provide a basis for developing the habit of lifelong learning.

In the next chapter we shall consider how educational resources might be enhanced in the U.S. and specifically how lifelong learning can be encouraged through a curriculum continuum extending from early childhood through the senior citizen years.

8

An Ability-Age Curriculum Continuum

[In] our generation man has begun to lose his faith that he can improve his lot through technical advance alone . . . The discrepancy between the development of natural science and that of . . . the social sciences is largely responsible for the disasters we are witnessing at present.

Men who are ignorant of the dynamic principles of social life can do less harm without chemistry which produces poison gas . . . and without the technology which enables them to destroy others from the air and allows them to replace bow and arrow with machine guns. Men who are incapable of constructive social life and use their scientific knowledge primarily to subjugate and exploit their fellow men do not deserve this knowledge.

—Alexander Franz

Since the end of the last century the basic organization of educational institutions in the U.S. has not changed appreciably, although there have been various modifications such as the development of the middle school. If we accept what scholars say lies ahead in the next century, then significant modifications will be needed in the U.S. educational system. In this chapter let us examine the changes in the organizational structure of the schools that probable future developments support. Changes should reflect the following:

1. The goals of instruction, insofar as possible, should be modified to reflect the images of the probable future and the knowledge deemed significant in content fields by scholars.
2. The school curriculum should provide opportunities for greater learner involvement in community, national, and international affairs.
3. The school structure should be more flexibly designed to accommodate the findings of psychologists, neurobiologists, and others whose research has a bearing on learning theory.

4. More consideration should be given to the educational implications of cross-disciplinary studies.

5. Development of curricula should take into account the broad range of human growth from birth to old age.

We now consider how these five changes might be phased into our educational resources by 1) a coordinated educational network, and 2) a seamless ability-age continuum of lifelong learning.

The Coordinated Educational Network

The coordinated educational network is an approach that should be carried out under the leadership of state departments of education or the U.S. Department of Education for developing cooperation among educational institutions and in sharing the funding. Such a network could be compared to a very large teachers' center of the sort that aroused considerable interest both in the U.S. and abroad during the late 1960s and 1970s.

Initially this network could be used to serve three different types of communities, (for example, a rural, urban, and suburban combination) with a resource center that would benefit all. Such a resource would provide for an interchange of ideas, personnel, and materials among the three communities. As suggested by the model in figure 12 the center would have resource persons (A) who coordinate the districts' curricular resources. Resource personnel (A1 through A6) would be scheduled to assist a specific community for a part of the school year and then shift to another community that requests them. The permanent director of the resource center would coordinate the allocation of personnel and resources to the school districts in the network. The model also illustrates how a resource center director can link facilities with adjacent resource centers in a given demographic area. This could be as large as a county, or even larger where the population is sparse.

The sharing of ideas, personnel, and materials among schools within a community, and between communities, states, and countries has a great deal to recommend it. Let us look at these potential advantages first at the local level, then at a broader view of the resource center concept.

Both research and observation indicate that much of the behavior of children is determined by their family relationships and home environments. As Wang [1] reports, several researchers also have found

---

[1]Margaret Wang, "Adaptive Instruction: Building on Diversity," *Theory into Practice*, Spring 1980, pp. 122-128.

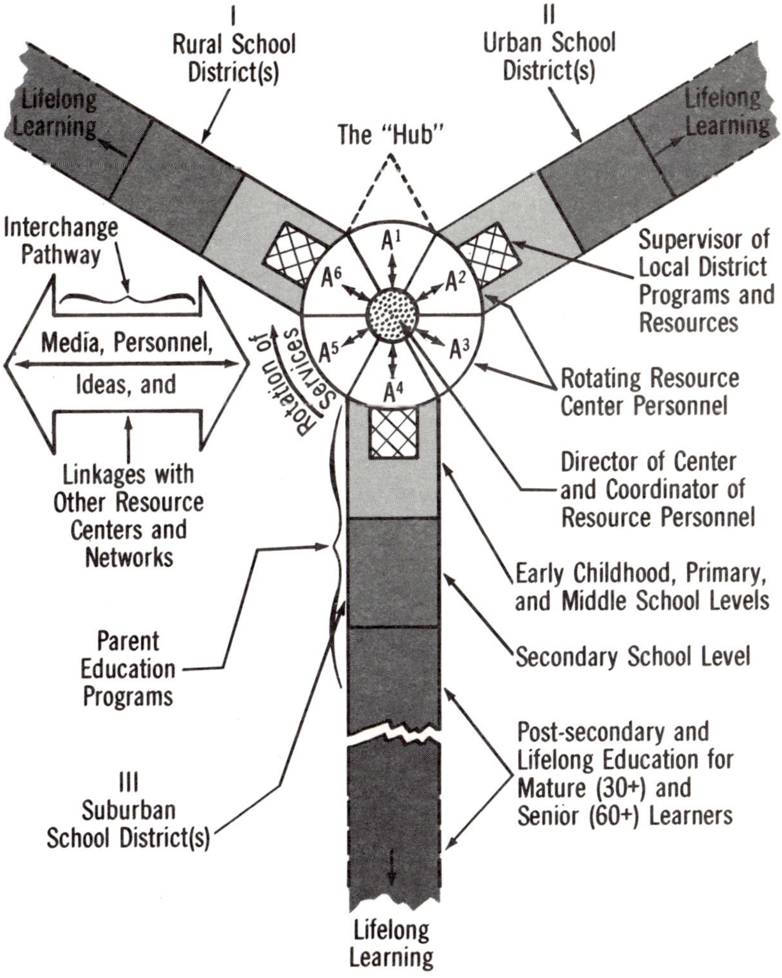

Participatory planning, cross-district research and curriculum development, as well as the sharing of resources and instructional strategies are implicit in the model.

Fig. 12. A model of coordinated educational network

that family involvement in the school program is a key factor affecting the social development and academic success of the individual child. The better informed and the more involved the families are with respect to curriculum content and their children's individual progress, the greater the likelihood is that their children will begin to achieve the goals set for them.

Parent-teacher involvement in resource center activities would need to be coordinated with respect to communication between schools of the same level (e.g., all the middle schools within the community or area) and between schools that enroll students at different age levels. Their cooperatively developed goals would determine the educational tone of the curriculum and instructional practices both in the individual school system and in the demographic area served by a given resource center.

To obtain access to an even greater number of ideas, personnel, and materials, as well as to increase the likelihood of exposure to varying subcultural groups, the resource center might (within reasonable limits) gradually be expanded as it became well established.

At the state or interstate level, large units representing, for example, agricultural states and industrial states could be organized to encourage interaction in a large region. Finally, at the international level three or more countries could establish a system of mutual support in improving education. Representation by industrialized and non-industrialized cultures might be a sensible combination at this level.

Let us also suggest that for some of the more mature secondary and postsecondary students there ought to be opportunities for involvement in cross-cultural exchanges. Such exchanges are not an entirely new idea at these levels. What is novel is expansion of this idea to younger students. Inter-school contacts at all levels have been widely supported in the area of sports for more than a century. There is no reason why such contacts could not be expanded beyond competitive sports activity to include cognitive and affective activities, such as short-term employment, work-and-study, travel, living for a semester with a family overseas, and so on.

The resource center. Because of costs, it is impractical for each school unit to set up its own resource center staffed by highly specialized personnel. With two or three districts sharing in the funding, the center concept begins to become viable. The director of the center makes the necessary contacts and coordinates the various human and material resources of the center and of the participating districts.

Each community should have its own local resource supervisor. Such a person would be familiar with the district's resources, arrange for parent input, be well acquainted with teachers, and know the characteristics of the study body and its educational needs. The local resource supervisor is the conduit for the input-output between the individual schools and the resource center personnel. These local community resource supervisors would form a consortium with the director of the area resource center. The director would be both the link between all the local community schools and the directors of other resource centers at the state and national levels.

The resource center is the hub from which educational specialists go to work with school personnel. In effect, the center would be a source of professional support for the improvement of virtually the entire educational environment of the community, from prenatal advice to parents to learning experiences for senior citizens. At each resource center, school personnel and community representatives could convene periodically to plan curricular and instructional acitivities and to evaluate work in progress. The planning and sharing of ideas at all of these levels should help the participating school to create a first-rate educational program.

The educational support system. The specialized resource personnel at the center could be rotated within the local area schools and sometimes assigned to other centers within a national and, perhaps eventually, an international network. Some of these persons might be recruited from university staff on sabbatical or from the supervisory staff of other communities. Others of equal importance might include qualified personnel from local business and industry or from professions such as nursing or law.

To illustrate how the educational support system might function, let us examine how resource specialists in human growth and development might operate. These persons provide such varied services as: 1) holding classes for parents on their roles and responsibilities during the prenatal and early childhood years; 2) working with teachers to develop the curriculum and instructional strategies for younger children; 3) training adolescents to serve as junior paraprofessionals at the nursery school level; 4) planning with community agencies such as day-care centers to improve their programs; 5) coordinating research within the schools in the area; 6) designing and staffing in-service work requested by teachers involved in early childhood education; 7) providing individual counsel for recently employed teachers; 8) preparing parents to supervise their children's homework, play periods, exposure to TV and stereo, and planning family experiences on holidays to make them more educational; and 9) developing ways in which school buildings and personnel can begin to serve the needs and interests of mature and senior learners.

After working over a given period of time in one community, the human development specialists would take on new responsibilities in a different community, and another specialist from a different field would become available for assignments dictated by local needs.

The use of itinerant specialists has several advantages. The participating school systems acquire the help of experts from different fields at an appreciably lower cost than if each maintained its own staff of specialists. Organizations such as parent groups or social agencies in the community also could receive the benefit of resource persons' expertise. Finally, the individual teacher would be provided with a continuing flow of professional advice from the resource personnel.

Certain advantages also exist for the personnel at a resource center: 1) career enrichment through exposure to practical situations; 2) contact with differing communities; 3) on-the-job training for advanced students in graduate school; 4) opportunities for conducting research; 5) increased flexibility in obtaining new educational input on a short-term basis at little or no cost; and 6) the opportunity to work with community agencies.

Another way in which a coordinated educational network could help to improve the efficiency of the cooperating educational institutions is through the sharing or exchange of physical resources. In this category are such things as sharing computer time and lending or exchanging the use of media equipment. Increasing physical resources should help to stretch the available funds at a time when economies are necessary. With an inventory of media and other equipment in the various schools served by a center, resource personnel could channel such resources to other schools on a rental or loan basis from the center.

Still another service of the resource center is organizing and coordinating student exchange programs. Such programs are complex to organize and can be costly. Through a network of schools coordinated through a resource center student exchange programs could be arranged more efficiently and economically. Eventually, on an international basis, students could visit or work in cooperating schools in other countries with the coordination of the visits or short-term work experiences handled by the resource center personnel.

The Ability-Age Continuum

We now turn to the second aspect of a future-focused organizational structure for our schools, a structure that accommodates a seamless lifelong ability-age curriculum that is based on the abilities and needs of individual learners rather than a lockstep graded school based on chronological age. We began by making the point that if schools are to deal with the concepts presented in chapters 3 and 4, some fundamental changes in the traditional organization of our schools will be necessary. To begin with, greater flexibility is needed if we are to encourage lifelong learning. Reasons for abandoning the traditional lockstep graded school structure include the following:

• Each person is unique with respect to physical, emotional, and cognitive development. In most graded schools, present practice is based on the assumption that children of a given age are more or less uniform in terms of intellectual and social performance. Actually, learners who are the same age vary enormously in performance; we should recognize this diversity.

• Learning is continuous; therefore educational facilities should be operated on a year-round basis. As it is, our school year schedule is based on the pretechnological needs of an agrarian society when students often worked in field and barn during the growing season. These conditions no longer prevail in most areas of the U.S. Furthermore, school facilities and personnel can be used more efficiently on a year-round basis. Learning does not need to take a summer vacation; nor does it stop after formal schooling terminates. Hence the arguments for a year-round school have become persuasive ones.

• Learning is inherently a lifelong experience and should, therefore, be facilitated by the use of educational resources on a lifelong basis.

The ability-age continuum for lifelong learning is an idea whose time has come. Not only is it supported by research findings, it is consistent with the need for persons of all ages to develop a knowledge of survival concepts for the future. Finally, it dovetails nicely with the idea of a coordinated, integrated, educational network.

Figure 13 visualizes the concept of an ability-age continuum that provides for lifelong learning. The horizontal line of small cubes represents the increasing age of the learner from the prenatal stage to age 70 and beyond. The two large cubes at the left represent a curriculum derived from images of the future and from real world learning resources, which, when properly utilized, can add a great deal of meaning to the future-oriented curriculum.

The figure suggests how the grouping and progress of learners is governed by individual maturity and readiness, by development and ability, not by chronological age. In such an organizational structure, those within any one learning group might span an age range of as many as five years. Let us examine this model in some detail to see how the curriculum can be designed in terms of what has been

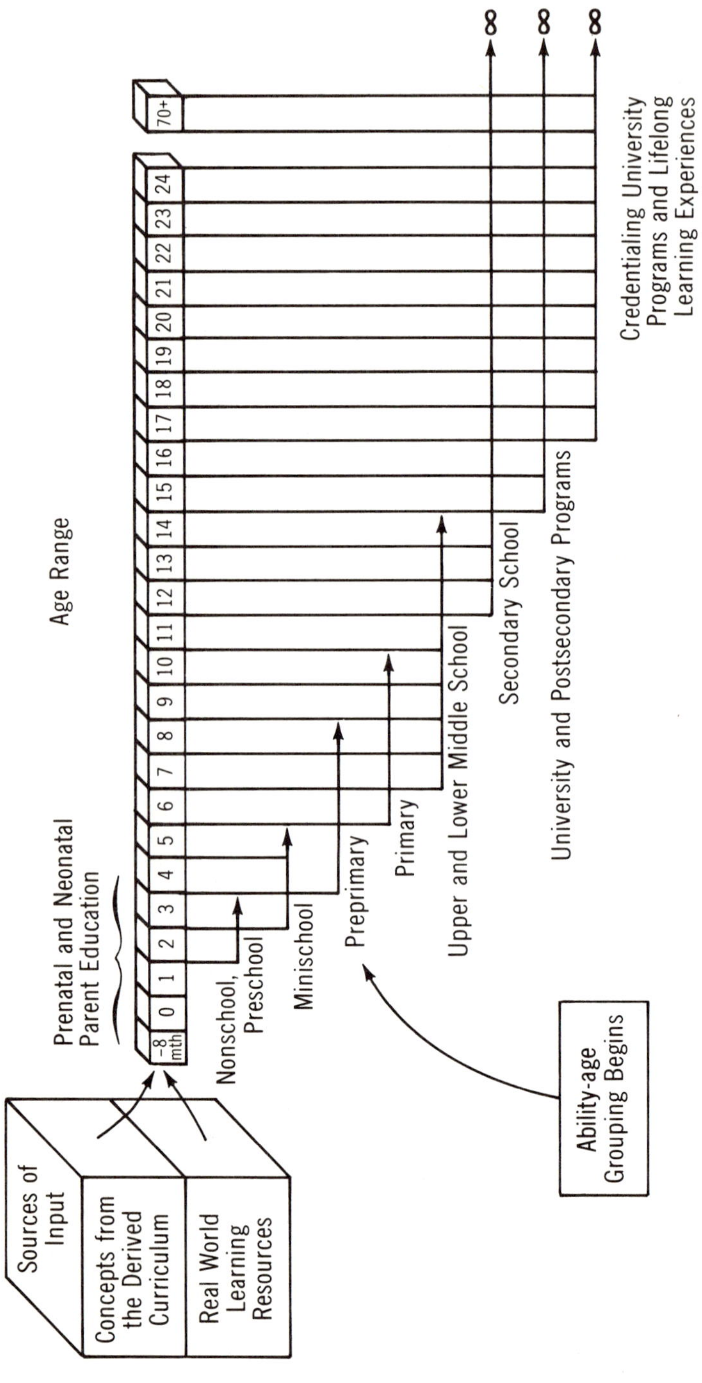

Fig. 13. The ability-age continuum

learned about human development, beginning with the prenatal period.

The prenatal period. During the past several decades evidence has accumulated that development during the years of infancy and early childhood has a substantial influence on subsequent intellectual, emotional, and social growth later in life. This insight with respect to the early years of life has led to increased efforts to extend education downward to include the early childhood years. Lately, that boundary has been pushed even farther to include the effects of the prenatal environment on human development. Research in this realm is still somewhat equivocal. However, certain physical and psychological aspects of pregnancy and of the fetal environment appear to affect subsequent mental and physical development throughout life. Information is becoming available on various fetal influences such as: the mother's health and diet; hereditary diseases; tobacco, alcohol, and drug consumption; physical exercise, travel, and work; contraceptive devices; medical care; type of labor and delivery; and intrauterine surgery performed before birth.

Prenatal and neonatal malnutrition also have been the object of a number of animal studies and some research with humans. Evidence is mounting that supports the thesis that malnutrition early in life can result both in physical harm and in brain damage that can affect individuals throughout life. Thus, educating expectant parents about the effects of variables in certain critical periods of gestation becomes an important goal in the lifelong education continuum in order to insure that learners get off to a good start. The prenatal and neonatal periods of life have too often been ignored in the past. More recently, a small but growing number of future parents have sought to inform themselves by reading books or by turning to health agencies or physicians for advice.

A learning continuum that begins in the early years of life has obvious advantages for the schools. If children are born with preventable handicaps, develop poorly, or are retarded in intellectual functioning, the remedial and compensatory programs they may require subsequently become an expensive undertaking for the schools. The need to reduce the number of children with preventable learning difficulties, coupled with the need to provide better protection for millions of young children and for the unborn, are compelling reasons for including prenatal education for parents as a part of the learning continuum.

The early childhood years. In general, the period from birth through the first years of formal schooling is referred to as early childhood. During this period several types of contact with the educational community occur in a lifelong learning continuum. Parents would obviously receive neonatal education; but there is also a place for such education for youth, particularly because of the substantial increase in teenage maternity. Also at this time, data about the physical and mental growth of the individual child could be compiled and put into computerized, cumulative, educational records that would accompany each child through adulthood. When ethically and professionally used, such data could be useful to teachers, counselors, and school physicians.

As our model shows, lifelong learning opportunities that begin during the neonatal stage would continue through the preschool stage. For the most part, this would be primarily in the home through contact with the infant's parents. Depending on the maturity of the child, enrollment in a nursery school or day-care center might begin somewhere around age three, under the auspices of the school system with teachers who are specialists in early childhood education.

When the child's social, physical, and intellectual development suggest that he or she is ready, there should be a transition to the pre-primary component. The learning climate at this pre-primary level would become more educational and less custodial than at previous levels, but readiness experiences rather than formal number or language skill learning would predominate.

As the model is intended to imply, for this and enusing transitions to higher stages of the continuum, the emphasis should be on helping individuals develop to an optimum point before proceeding onward to the next stage of their educational experiences. A few children will move at a very fast pace through these stages and can be placed in more academically demanding environments. Others will need to invest more time at a given level. These levels for learning, we repeat, would not be based on chronological age per se but on such individual factors as interest, developmental level, social maturity, and learning style—factors that research indicates are more important indices of potential for cognitive growth than is a child's age. The groups emerging from such a placement process would span several age levels, but their level of performance would be more homogeneous than in the graded school. Also, with suitable guidance from the teacher, ability-age grouping should facilitate the earlier acceptance of younger learners' participation in school activities such as athletic events, dramatics, or presentations for parents when a unit of study draws to a close.

The last of the transitions during the early childhood years is to the primary level. At this point the students begin to be exposed to the systematic study of basic skills such as reading, mathematics, and spelling, which will provide the foundation for most of their subsequent formal and informal education.

The middle school period. In the middle school, once again, the students would follow a personalized path through the continuum and move at their own rate of social and academic progress, thus eliminating the need for retention of slower learning children or of "skipping" more rapid learners a grade. The personalized path for each student obviously would increase the age range beyond that now found in the middle school; a relative decrease in ability range also would occur. These practices also should help to reduce the frustration of trying to cope with children of the same chronological age, who may vary as much as five or six years in their standardized test scores, yet are expected to meet the same requirements in an identical curriculum.[2]

Middle school learning experiences in the continuum will focus on the wider application of skills and processes introduced in primary school. Specific subject matter areas, such as science and the social studies, become more distinct. Community involvement and action or service learning should also increase sharply at this level. Experiences in the real world would provide motivation for educational activities that, hopefully, would counteract the endemic student malaise that often begins at this age and continues throughout the rest of their schooling.[3]

The secondary school level. As students become ready for the more highly structured content in the secondary school, they will continue their uninterrupted progress on the ability-age continuum. Several modifications in traditional organization are needed at this level to accommodate the concepts of a seamless curriculum continuum and the changing psychological climate of secondary schools.

One needed change is the elimination of rigid demarcations between subject matter areas and a movement toward interdisciplinary approaches. This becomes possible through teaching partnerships where two or more teachers work together to insure that the academic quality of instruction remains high. Recall that an inter-

---

[2]Readers who are familiar with the work of Benjamin S. Bloom will recognize that the personalized ability-age concept developed here is based on his mastery learning thesis that a large majority of children, perhaps 90%, can reach acceptable levels of performance if they are given sufficient time in which to do so.

[3]For detailed models of a school's organizational structure in an ability-age continuum see Harold G. Shane, *The Educational Significance of the Future*, pp. 68-76. For models of school organization for implementing action and service learning, see Shane, *Curriculum Change Toward the 21st Century*, pp. 111-127. (Full references appear in the bibliography.)

disciplinary approach in secondary schools clearly was implied or explicitely recommended by many participants in our study. A second desirable change would be discarding the semester structure of the school, at least in part, so that learning is continuous. This is possible by making better use of programmed materials and computerized instruction. A third point emphasized in previous chapters is that of instilling desirable ecological attitudes, a better understanding of human interdependence, and an enhanced appreciation for the values associated with empathic interpersonal relationships. A fourth change is one that has been a major theme of this monograph; namely, the infusion of real world experiences into the secondary curriculum. The notion of the paracurriculum, which involves out-of-school work experience, has been discussed in *The Educational Significance of the Future*[4] and deserves reexamination here as an approach to infusing greater social and economic meaning into the secondary school setting. These contacts can supplant some in-school experiences and supplement vocational education activities. This type of program, for which the school serves as a broker, would both modify the climate of learning and provide a sensible transition to post-secondary education or the world of work.

Recurrent education. An ability-age continuum augments most present day schooling not only by extending downward to the prenatal period but also by providing learning experiences for people throughout their life cycle. Firsthand work experiences, which have long been a part of some collegiate academic programs, probably could be extended further to include student exchanges, internships, and apprenticeships at the international level. The flexibility of scheduling entry and reentry has been worked out successfully in some institutions of higher learning but needs to be more widely implemented.

Alternatives to augment, not to replace, the conventional university are being explored, and the trend should be encouraged. One innovative example of the late 1960s and early 1970s is Great Britain's highly successful Open University, a creative approach to a baccalaureate degree or other forms of self improvement through television, periodic regional seminars, and materials especially prepared by experts. Another illustration is the educational programs for men and women overseas in the armed services. More than 20 of these educational centers were open during the 1970s in Europe alone.

As Roberto Vacca and others on our panel noted, we need to devise more ways of informing and teaching adults by television. Tele-

[4]Harold G. Shane, *The Educational Significance of the Future* (Bloomington, Ind.: Phi Delta Kappa, 1973), pp. 71-76.

vision has potential for providing mass higher education without the financial expense of physical attendance at an institution. Televised or radio courses, either for credit or for informative purposes, need not begin only at the postsecondary level; they also could be used with learners of any background, including the world's millions who neither can read nor write.

In addition to increasing the scope and quality of opportunities for postsecondary education, more programs are needed in all types of institutions that recognize the needs of mature adults. Recurrent education should include the phase-in of offerings that are pertinent to the interests of the mature and senior learner and which vary in length from brief seminars to conventional courses.

Summary

Even though the object of our study was to inventory the concepts that young learners need to grasp if they are to survive successfully in the future, our interviews clearly indicated that *all* people everywhere must be involved in acquiring survival skills for a period that seems certain to be one of prolonged turmoil.

Many scholars in the sciences emphasized the significance of a lifelong plan for educating the world's peoples. Some of the more pertinent comments on this subject during our many dialogues were made by Harold Dent, professor emeritus at the University of London, and are presented here as an appropriate ending for chapter 8:

> Students should realize that education is a lifelong process, continuous from birth to death; that it begins in the home, whose primary function is to initiate the child into the attitudes, mode of living, and morals of the society, and to inculcate a due respect for other cultures . . . .
>
> As for schooling, it is an essential supplement, but only a supplement, to the education given by home and society. Its function is to assist in laying the foundations of some of the basic skills required for successful living, and to create a mind that is active, purposeful, and flexible. But we must remember that the schooling we receive in childhood and adolescence is but the beginning of the continued learning experiences that people everywhere need as we strive to cope with the many better tomorrows that I hope the human race may experience.

9

Epilogue: The Importance of Education in Coming Decades

If you do not think about the future, you cannot have one.
—John Galsworthy

From the concepts gleaned from scholars involved in our study, we know that the learning process, broadly conceived to include both schooling and lifelong education, will play a significant role in the years ahead. What both the natural and social sciences have to suggest as new directions for U.S. education is a blend of inquiry, art, and philosophy. The sciences are, first of all, *methods of inquiry*. They also bring order out of enormous quantities of data, a process that transmutes them to *arts*. Finally, the sciences are *philosophies* in the sense that they bring us doctrines of enlightenment and vision.[1]

What summarizing statements can be made then, on the basis of our interview data, about the nature of education for survival and humane living and about the prospects for worldwide changes in teaching and learning? For one thing, as humans move toward a new millennium they could, like dinosaurs or mammoths, become transient guests on this globe unless their social wisdom can match and overcome their ingenuity in creating technologically ingenious but dangerous weapons, toxic chemicals, and nuclear waste. The role of education in modifying this situation needs no elaboration! Survival skills must be in the curriculum.

Second, for the foreseeable future what is taught in schools or through any educational media must help us cope with the fact that in *all* nations there are many persons who continue to disregard the French "Declaration of the Rights of Man." Thus, billions have been

[1]For a nicely etched elaboration of this point, see Will and Ariel Durant, *The Lessons of History* (New York: Simon and Schuster, 1968), p. 12.

born to an estate that is neither free, nor equal, nor characterized by *fraternité*.

Third, we can infer from the scholars who probe our environment and study our world cultures that one of the challenges to learning in our era is to remove, or at least begin to diminish, the present deep uncertainty as to the most viable directions in which to move if we are to achieve a decent, humane way of living. Heretofore, in Teilhard de Chardin's words, ". . . the workers and the disinherited accepted without reflection the lot which kept them in servitude . . ."[2] Now we must begin to understand that civilization is:

> . . . a co-operative product, that nearly all people have contributed to it; it is our common heritage and debt; and that the civilized soul will reveal itself in treating every man and woman, however lowly, as a member of these creative and contributory groups.[3]

Life has always been—and still is—competitive and selective. A strong case probably can be made for leaving it that way! As Garrett Hardin argues, "What would the [U.S.] educational system produce if we saw to it that competitive excellence was not rewarded?"[4] However, social inequalities in the past 30 to 40 years have become even greater. Therefore, social justice must be improved so that a given individual can compete on a somewhat even basis through equitable access to education.

This leads to a fourth generalization; namely, that education should be directed at the establishment of new moral bases. Whether such moral bases be metaphysical or a secular "religion of humanity" is irrelevant, as long as they help us to differentiate between good and evil and help us to meet the cruel and harsh tests which almost certainly lie ahead.

Finally, our natural and social scientists spoke, with occasional eloquence due to their deep concern, of the need for understanding that any quest for economic advantage that does harm to the general welfare will serve to heighten the worldwide turbulence that already exists in the early 1980s.

Now let us move on to review and synthesize some of the specific educational directions, policies, and practices that the thinking of our 132 scholars appears to support.

---

[2]Teilhard de Chardin, *The Phenomenon of Man* (London and Glasgow: William Collins and Sons, Ltd., 1952), p. 230.

[3]The Durants, ibid., p. 31.

[4]Garrett Hardin, *Promethean Ethics* (Seattle: University of Washington Press, 1980), p. 38.

Educational Directions for the 1980s: Some Recommendations

General suggestions. Since the need for lifelong learning was repeatedly mentioned in earlier chapters, most of the points that follow pertain to both formal and informal education which extend from the child's early years to the mastery of developmental tasks of advanced maturity.

1. In a highly complex world, the curriculum for living in a new millennium should be derived from carefully developed images of the future, which learners young and old are inheriting from the past and the present.

2. The idea that equal opportunity in education means the same for everyone ought to be reexamined. Because of the differences that exist among learners of every age, the content, methods, and organization of the curriculum should be adapted to the gradations in the levels of human development. Phrased in another way, good learning is personalized learning. Furthermore, because of rapid technological, social, and cultural change and the opportunities they often create, "personalization" should not be interpreted to mean that learners are groomed for and locked into predetermined life roles selected by teachers. Such lock-ins may not be in their best interests and also might lead to careers for which some students have no talent.

3. Education, including schooling, should serve to *increase* rather than to decrease human differences in one's ability to contribute to society. Unique minds and rare talents must be cultivated and encouraged so that they can help to build better tomorrows. An exception to this generalization is the need for learning experiences to *decrease* human differences with respect to the ability to *communicate* more clearly.

4. Learners frequently need to be protected from the effects of "junk information" that the media, especially television, sometimes provide. The scope of the problem is reflected in data cited by Neil Postman in 1981 suggesting that well over a half-million children in the U.S. are watching late TV shows between midnight and 2:00 A.M. on a given night![5]

5. Industrially developed nations now strive to provide basic security through free or inexpensive health and welfare services. As a result, many U.S. youth no longer have the motivation to work created by an empty stomach. At the same time, some astute young people sense that there is no longer enough affluence to go around as we approach the limits of the earth's carrying capacity. One result is that because many people, young and old, fear neither hunger nor

---

[5]Neil Postman, "The Day Our Children Disappear: Predictions of a Media Ecologist," *Phi Delta Kappan*, January 1981, pp. 382-386.

anticipate great material improvement in their lives, education must seek new and worthy means of motivating them. In serving this end, curriculum planning should consider jobs for tomorrow and what the changing workplace will demand.

6. In many sections of the globe, carefully planned changes in general education are needed to improve the status of women. As the U.N.'s Helvi Sipilä put it, "... unless we take seriously the fate of women, I don't think we can solve many other problems: population, food shortage, illiteracy, abandoned children, unemployment, and mass poverty."[6]

7. As a corollary of the point above, the need to improve the status of women suggests that provisions for prenatal care need to be improved and that universal, childhood education, as early as age two or three, should become an integral component of the lifelong educational continuum in order to reduce or to prevent learning problems later in children's lives.

8. Anthropologists point out that in a hunting culture the hunt itself is the teacher. By the same token, in a highly organized society, the society itself should be the teacher. This concept is one that James Coleman and Alvin Toffler have labeled "action" and "service" learning—educational experiences that are sponsored or brokered by the school but extend beyond its walls into the wider community.

9. Because of contemporary changes in the nature and structure of family life, traditional patterns of home-school and parent-teacher relationships will require further study and modification. Both greater parental acceptance of responsibility and more flexible school programs seem desirable, though both will have to be mediated by a given culture and its ethos.

Curriculum organization. How knowledge is best structured, what learning is of most worth, and how it is best acquired have been topics of debate for centuries. It is not our purpose here to enter into this controversial arena. Rather, we shall endeavor to propose a few of the practices and to inventory some of the broad concepts of *lifelong learning* that the probable future will require in view of unsettling political developments, uncertain economic conditions, and the new social systems that are piecing themselves together into the interstices of older social structures. In this context at least five generalizations regarding curriculum organization seem justified:

10. Learning, regardless of how it is acquired, can no longer be conceived as a mechanical process. It is not something that can be put together as plumbers, carpenters, and masons put a house together. Social change and the prospect of a society characterized by

[6]In a conversation with one of the writers.

dynamic contraction in the use of resources and by developments in microelectronics and robotics simply do not lend themselves to the rigidity of traditional approaches to the curriculum.

11. Since the swift flow of events that can be anticipated in the next 20 years promises to foreclose certain options, reforms both in educational opportunities and in structure of education need to be made rapidly. This is particularly true of the continuing education of adults, who are already participating in decision making in their communities.

12. Except for some forms of compensatory financial support distributed by central government agencies (support needed to insure equitable learning opportunities), the organization and administration of education should be based on local control and local decisions so that those persons most acquainted with the immediate community's needs, with respect to schooling the young and the continuing education of all, can deploy the resources available to meet them.

13. At the transnational level, organizational practices should make more use of educational systems and technologies as in Britain's Open University. Radio and television, if kept free of political influence and of the propaganda of special interest groups, can make significant contributions to the sharing of knowledge and ideas among semiliterate as well as literate populations.

14. While technology is of proven value in performing certain instructional tasks, the use of such powerful educational agents as television must be made more consonant with the best human values and traditions. We reiterate that care must be exercised by persons in the teaching profession to reduce the likelihood that unscrupulous elements in the population will continue to use the media to further their ambitions.

Methods and curriculum content. In this section we present certain generalizations on instructional methods and curriculum content with which this study has been concerned.

15. The content of the U.S. curriculum and the methods of instruction employed should not indoctrinate the learner with past dogmas, many of which may become untenable or of dubious value for tomorrow's world. However, our past should not be ignored as a source of information since, as Santayana once noted, those who forget the past are condemned to relive it.

16. In view of human diversity, the good curriculum should neither turn out programmed pupils nor seek to clone a uniform student product. Instructional methods will vary from one learner to another throughout life, because learners of the same chronological age differ enormously in developmental age. Those who learn rapidly should encounter instruction that is interesting and intel-

lectually demanding. Slower learners should not be exposed to pressures that are unreasonable for them. The lifelong, seamless learning continuum concept presented in chapter 8 is offered as a *problem-preventing* approach to learning that is designed to reduce and eventually to eliminate the need for compensatory education. In such a continuum special care should be given to defining the criteria governing success and failure at any given time, since wide differences in performance should be expected from both children and adult learners.

17. Trends in the social sciences, with their complexity and adumbrations, make it particularly important for the curriculum to provide basic communication skills, including competence in visual literacy. We also conclude from our study that an understanding of at least one foreign language is desirable for many learners. It goes without saying that the listening and mathematical skills needed for the communication of ideas are more indispensable than ever. Also, particular attention should be given to helping persons in a wide age range to distinguish between shoddy and ethical advertising, to recognize political double-talk, and to discount propaganda in its various forms.

18. In the process of improving learning through curriculum changes, the present-day proliferation of elective subjects and options should be reexamined. Discussion-discovery or heuristic methods have certain well-attested values. However, if the scholarly opinions from our scientists are valid, there also are times when learners need to be *taught* certain content if they are to become informed persons. The human heritage cannot be acquired exclusively through so-called group processes, heuristic strategies, and interaction!

19. The content of instruction should be designed to reduce the harsh realities of the current era by focusing, when appropriate, on peaceful ways of achieving changes needed to improve the human community. Furthermore, because of the need for learners of all ages to anticipate, comprehend, and cope with complex relationships, interdisciplinary learnings need to be incorporated into a general education.

20. Because, within limits, humans create the future, the idea of alternative futures and how to choose among them to serve the world's good should be a component of a future-oriented curriculum.

21. Points 19 and 20 above call to mind the need for curriculum content and instructional practices that direct attention to understanding the prevailing threats to the biosphere and to understanding the human geography of the earth's cultures.

22. Curricular innovations and alternative educational practices often have been short-lived, little more than the ephemeral "may-

flies" of the educational world. Furthermore, changes in educational practice have not always reflected our increased knowledge of human growth and development. In the next two decades this knowledge must be applied more thoroughly and, insofar as possible, on an international scale. Changes within America's boundaries alone are not sufficient when educational needs are worldwide.

Choosing among Conflicting Curriculum Conceptions

In chapter 1 we outlined the spectrum of curriculum choices. These range from regressive choices, a return to discarded values and practices, to a regenerative alternative involving methodical transformation of schools in the U.S. In view of the above educational directions for the 1980s, some choice seems almost inevitable. It probably will be the eclectic option, one that uses the best positive aspects of all five of the alternatives that were presented.

Indeed, there is much to support the eclectic option for a future-focused curriculum. The cultural heritage from the past, represented by the durable perennialist choice, cannot be discarded. At the same time, there are many positive aspects of U.S. education today that should be retained as noted by Ralph Tyler[7] in his 1981 essay on academic performance. What is working well in the curriculum should be retained.

Nor is it mere conciliatory rhetoric to point out that there is a place for the liberal position with its psychosocial, humanistic view of the learner, and for the experimental position that, during the 20th century, has helped to enrich to teaching profession through the work of such able practitioners as Helen Parkhurst, Flora Cook, Carleton W. Washburne, and the staff of the *Eight Year Study* conducted by the Progressive Education Association. Although the writers have great respect for the regenerative curriculum conception, it is simple common sense to recognize that an all-out drive to remodel U.S. education totally in the short-term future is impossible. Changes during the next decade that will endure are likely to be made by those who already are working within the established educational community. This leaves us with the eclectic choice that permits the educator to create a desirable amalgam of the several virtues of all the curriculum conceptions. This would be an educational position that lies somewhere between John Fisher's "volcanic" and "coral reef" changes described earlier.

In summary, the 22 educational directions above point to the need for a reasonably paced and continuous educational transformation

[7]See Ralph W. Tyler, "The U.S. versus the World: A Comparison of Educational Performance," *Phi Delta Kappan*, January 1981, pp. 307-310.

based on the best features of past and present practices recast and supplemented by the demands that the scholars we interviewed believe the future will impose.

Concluding Comment

Many of our data were gloomy and many of our extended dialogues with scholars were pessimistic, but our optimism tended to grow slowly and steadily during the 18 months of our inquiry. One reason for our generally sanguine attitudes is the fact that we are now better aware of what the world of tomorrow may be like and what we must do for survival and for a decent existence. The awareness we found among the scholars was worldwide, and so was their conviction that the planet could be put in order. Furthermore, we are learning to adapt ourselves to the arrival of tomorrow; we are no longer paralyzed by what Alvin Toffler called future shock. We can even, within limits, "create" the future as was demonstrated by moon landings, human rights legislation, and the clean-up of waterways that began to be polluted as far back as the 18th century.

In addition, in many parts of the world enormous natural resources remain untapped. We need only to show greater prudence in using them wisely. And we have time—time reaching into the new millennium—to prove that disturbing trends and alarming past developments need not be a preview of human destiny. Rather, they should serve as a distant early warning, alerting us to the need for better ecological behavior patterns than those that have prevailed in the past. In the future we can anticipate that developments yet to come in scientific knowledge and technology are trump cards remaining in our hands. Our task is to play these cards wisely!

Finally, humans have a great track record, having survived diseases, famines, floods, and earthquakes, as well as man-made catastrophes. And the people on this planet have made great progress since 1900: from combatting disease to a new mastery of the elements; from the Wright brothers' brief flight to exploration of the outer space; from a view of women and blacks as human chattel to truly great gains in human rights for these groups.

Much of the disturbing bad news can be countered with good news because people are no longer, like ants crawling on a tapestry, able to see only a tiny bit of the large picture woven into the fabric around them. We can stand back and take a *Weltanschauung*, a world view, of the globe in all its aspects. Our months of inquiry have left us believing that people will continue to take the long view, to make the right decisions, and to take the right actions for the right reasons more often in the future than in the past.

Appendix A
Backgrounds and Procedures of the Study

Until the 20th century, schooling in the U.S. and in most parts of the industrialized world was a supplement to education. Childhood was brief and preadolescents quickly became a part of the predominantly rural work force.[1] Boys acquired the arts of husbandry as they worked the fields with fathers or neighbors. Girls learned the household arts by practicing them at their mothers' sides. Trades and skills were mastered through apprenticeships on the job, in mill and mine, in farm and forest, in smithy and in shop.

In effect, education—what one needed to know to survive and prosper—was a part of living. Schooling was usually limited to the elementary level and provided basic skills; black-and-white, Currier-and-Ives, moral values; and physical and mental discipline.[2]

The changing status of the young. As the industrial world became more complex with assembly lines and mechanized agricultural equipment, there was less need for young males in the fields. With more production and distribution of food supplies, there was less need for young females in the home to preserve fruit and vegetables.

One outcome of the decline in need for child labor was the burgeoning of our secondary school enrollment. A high school education began to become commonplace after World War I. Attending high school tended to keep youth off the labor market, but it also helped youth to acquire some of the vocational skills prerequisite to employment in business and industry.

Another outcome was the growing segregation of the young into a peer culture that divorced them from participation in the adult activities that previously had served as a transition to the adult world. By the 1920s William H. Kilpatrick was calling for educational changes designed to cope with social and economic mutations occurring in the U.S.[3] The 1930s witnessed some of

[1]At the time of the first U.S. Census, approximately 95% of the population lived in rural areas. By 1980, only about 5% were engaged in farming.

[2]As late as 1940, U.S. Census records show that over half of the adult population had not completed elementary school.

[3]William H. Kilpatrick, *Education for a Changing Civilization* (New York: Macmillan, 1926).

the pioneering efforts to compensate for the loss of important educational experiences caused by the widening gap between the school and the real world.

Early efforts at youth community involvement. One of the pioneers in the quest for ways of creating real world challenge for youth was Paul R. Hanna, who believed that "*cooperative activities for community improvement* form the vision of the best education yet conceived."[4] His *Youth Serves the Community* (1936) recorded some of the efforts being made in the U.S. and overseas to create learning experiences that paralleled, complemented, and enriched schooling. In the parlance of the times, the community involvement Hanna described was known as "socially useful work," the purpose of which was 1) to provide an education for living in a democratic society and a changing world, 2) to make clear through education that we are now living in an interdependent world, and 3) to provide an education through which old and young together work to bring about a better society in the U.S.[5]

Among the socially useful work activities for youth were public safety, civic beauty, community health, agricultural and industrial improvement, civic arts, local history, surveys and inventories, and protection of resources. It is important to note in retrospect how widespread the interest in meaningful involvement of children and youth had become in the pre-World War II, Great Depression years. More than 150 specific ventures are listed in Hanna's book.

The community school concept. Also, during the 1930s, there was a movement within the schools analogous to socially useful work. This movement was designed to create socially significant educational programs that extended beyond the school walls, where many felt the young had been kept in quarantine. This was the community school movement. Kilpatrick offers a rationale for the community school when he stated:

> . . . that life and learning are more intimately interrelated than most people have hitherto thought, and accordingly that study and learning have in them more of the active and interactive quality that characterize life—and life in society—than most schools and school people have been willing to recognize.[6]

The community school in its day was not unlike many of the alternative or "open" schools of the 1970s and 1980s which carried on the legacy of progressive education in the 1930s. A good description of these schools is found in Elsie Clapp's *Community Schools in Action* where in the foreword, John Dewey writes that there are:

> . . . schools in our country which have made a reality out of theories about the social function of schools—by creating a school to which

---

[4]From the Introduction in Paul R. Hanna, *Youth Serves the Community* (New York: D. Appleton-Century 1936). Italics in original.

[5]Ibid., pp. 12-13.

[6]William H. Kilpatrick, "Principles of Community Learning," in Samuel Everett, ed., *The Community School* (New York: D. Appleton-Century, 1938), p. 1.

> Lincoln's words about democratic government apply: a school not only for, but of and by the community . . . .[7]

One more historically interesting volume that describes early attempts to build a spirit of community is *Were We Guinea Pigs?*[8] written by 55 graduating seniors in the Class of 1938 at the Ohio State University Campus School. The book describes how education can be an integral part of a larger society than the school itself, especially in the chapters, "Learning About Living" and "Governing Ourselves."

Action and service learning. So-called child-centered learning languished during World War II and during the 1950s, an era when education was under attack by such writers as Arthur Bestor. The "quest for excellence" following the launching of Sputnik in 1957 preoccupied education for much of the next decade. So did concern for the disadvantaged, the war on poverty, and later, the back-to-basics movement.

Nonetheless, more than 35 years after Hanna compiled *Youth Serves the Community*, the concept of socially useful work was still very much alive. In *Learning for Tomorrow*[9] Alvin Toffler and his associates repeatedly emphasized the importance of service learning, a contemporary variant of Hanna's community service. Further support and dignity were lent to both service and action learning, i.e., firsthand, off-campus experiences in *Youth: Transition to Adulthood*.[10] This influential volume, prepared in the mid-1970s under the chairmanship of James S. Coleman, was a report of the Panel on Youth of the President's Science Advisory Committee. In a subsequent conversation with the writer, Coleman noted that "Our recommendations included both the possibility of some kind of responsible productive (off-campus) work throughout the period of high school and the period of college . . . and . . . a full-time period of responsible work during an intervening year between high school and college.[11] The task of finding meaningful work experiences for children and youth, experiences which once were a part of the family-community living, remains a difficult one.

Walkabout. In the May 1974 issue of the *Phi Delta Kappan*, one of the most promising approaches to the transition from youth to the adult world was proposed by Maurice Gibbons in his provocative essay, "Walkabout." Gibbons was motivated to write his article after viewing the Australian film of the same name, which concerns the rite of passage from childhood to adulthood devised by Australian aborigines. In Gibbons' words, it is "a six-month-long endurance test during which [the young aborigine] must survive

---

[7]Elsie Ripley Clapp, *Community Schools in Action* (New York: Viking Press, 1939), p. viii.

[8]The Class of 1938, *Were We Guinea Pigs?* (New York: Henry Holt and Company, 1938).

[9]Alvin Toffler, ed., *Learning for Tomorrow* (New York: Random House, 1974).

[10]James S. Coleman, et al., *Youth: Transition to Adulthood* (Chicago: University of Chicago Press, 1974).

[11]Reported in *Today's Education*, March-April, 1975, pp. 74-80.

in the wilderness and return to his tribe an adult, or die in the attempt." In the article Gibbons makes some uncomfortable comparisons between the aborigines' and our rites of passage:

> . . . When the aborigine returns, his readiness and worth have been clearly demonstrated to him and to his tribe. They need him. He is their hope for the future. It is a moment worth celebrating. What, I wonder, would an alien humanoid conclude about adulthood in our society if he had to make his deductions from a graduation ceremony announcing students' maturity: speeches, a parade of candidates—with readings from their yearbook descriptions—a formal dinner, expensive clothes and cars, graduates over here, adults over there, all-night parties, occasional drunkenness and sexual experience or flirtation with it, and spray-painting "Grad '74" on a bridge or building. For many it is a memorable occasion—a pageant for parents, a good time for the students. But what is the message in this celebration at this most important moment of school life and in this most important shared community experience? What values does it promote? What is it saying about 12 years of school experience? The achievement of what goals is being celebrated? What is it teaching about adulthood? How is it contributing to a sense of community? What pleasures and sources of challenge and fulfillment does it encourage the young to pursue? And if our alien humanoid could look into the students' deepest thoughts, what would he conclude about their sense of readiness to live full and independent lives, to direct their own growth, to contribute to society, and to deal with the issues that confront us as a world—perhaps a universe—citizenry? I think his unprejudiced conclusion would horrify us.[12]

Gibbons goes on to point out that a walkabout type of experience could provide a useful model in redesigning our own rites of passage. While he would not subject youth to spend six months in the desert or the wilderness, he asks, "*What would an appropriate and challenging walkabout for students in our society be like?*"

Exploring new paths to maturity. In response to Gibbons' question, Phi Delta Kappa set up a Task Force on Compulsory Education and Transitions for Youth in 1974. The walkabout concept was developed by the task force with funding from the Lilly Endowment for use by schools contemplating action and service learning opportunities for their students. The task force also published a report that served as platform statement for reform of secondary education.[13]

Our present report, *Educating For a New Millennium* continues the exploration of ways in which, in a spirit of growing community, our schools can share with learners of all ages the coping and survival skills, that is, the guidelines to humane, mature living for today and for the decades which lie ahead.

---

[12]Maurice Gibbons, "Walkabout: Searching for the Right Passage from Childhood and School," *Phi Delta Kappan*, May 1974, pp. 597.

[13]Maurice Gibbons, *The New Secondary Education* (A Phi Delta Kappa Task Force Report, Bloomington, Ind.: Phi Delta Kappa, 1976).

Survival skills for tomorrow: the concept inventory. Chapters 2 and 3 sought to explain basic concepts which a large panel of distinguished scholars in the natural and social sciences deemed most important for young learners to grasp as they move toward adulthood. Real world experiences will be required to put these concepts into action in order to help our young to live full, independent lives in the future. The precepts in our derived curriculum described in chapter 7 should serve to direct this action. The concept inventory suggests substantive content and basic ideas to be considered by those involved in curriculum development.

Procedures for the Study

Prospective participants to be interviewed for this study were identified by sending a questionnaire and a descriptive statement of the project to name chair professors and a few top-ranking university administrators in the U.S. and overseas. Informal contacts also were made with some well-known futurists and leaders of educational associations to see if they would note any deficiencies or oversights in the study. Those contacted were Lester R. Brown, president of Worldwatch; Edward Cornish, president of World Future Society and publisher of *The Futurist*, and his wife, Sally Cornish; Eleanora Masini of the Pontifical Gregoriana University in Rome (Dr. Masini was also one of those interviewed for the study); Chris Dede of the National Institute of Education; Owen Kiernan and Scott Thomson of the National Association of Secondary School Principals; Paul Salmon of the American Association of School Administrators; William Pharis of the National Association of Elementary School Principals; and Walter Graves, former editor of the National Education Association journal, *Today's Education*.

Each person contacted was asked for his or her opinions about the value of the study and for their recommendations of scholars to be interviewed. Some name chair professors were asked to participate in the interviews as well as to recommend others. Through this process an attempt was made to identify a widening circle of scholars whose work was most respected in the natural and social sciences.

Those disciplines identified for inclusion in the natural sciences were chemistry, physics, geology and biology. The social science disciplines included were anthropology, economics, political science, sociology, psychology, and linguistics. Inquiries were limited to scholars in the natural and social sciences at the outset, but a few exceptions were made later to include the views of theologians, lawyers, and criminologists.

Participants were selected and invited for interviews on the basis of the following criteria: contributions to research; importance of their writings; opinions of their colleagues; frequency of mention in the questionnaires; listing in *Who's Who in America*, *International Biographical Dictionary*, and *National Academy of Arts and Sciences*; adequate representation of European, North American, Latin American, and Asian scholars with a geographical spread within each of these continents; multiethnic diversity; adequate representation of female participants; and a representative number of scholars from each of the disciplines identified in the natural and social sciences. All participants were asked to indicate what concepts they deemed most important for our youth to grasp for purposes of survival, coping, and civilized living as we approach the year 2000.

Letters of invitation for interviews were sent to 298 prospective participants in three successive mailings. One hundred and thirty-two interviews were conducted during the course of the study.

All those interviewed received a project description and exemplary model of some concepts,[14] not from their own area of expertise, well in advance of the interview. When possible, face-to-face interviews were conducted. The others were interviewed by appointment over the telephone. About 10 panelists responded so fully to the questionnaire that interviews were not necessary. The project director, project associate, and project assistant conducted the interviews, which were tape-recorded and transcribed later for purposes of analysis.

The analysis of responses was made within each of the disciplines, within the broader categories of the natural and social sciences, and across all areas on the basis of similarity of concepts mentioned. Summary statements of the concepts mentioned were compiled by the project director and his associates.

Project personnel then used discussions with teachers and curriculum coordinators, as well as their own expertise, to outline a curriculum of survival skills for the next quarter century based on the concepts gleaned from the scholars' interviews.

---

[14]*Concept*, for purposes of our inquiry, refers to a generalized idea based on scholarly opinion and/or factual information. It was assumed that the concept inventory could serve as a foundation for curriculum planning to some extent, as a referent in the selection of the content of instruction, and as a basis for identifying problem-solving skills.

Appendix B
Panel of Scholars Participating in the Project

Name	Area of Expertise	Affiliation
Philip H. Abelson	Geology	American Association for the Advancement of Science, Washington, D.C.
Sabino Acquaviva	Sociology	University of Padua, Padua, Italy
Warren E. Adam	Economics	Intermediate Technology Development Group Ltd., London, England
Marvin Aliske	Political Science	Arizona State University
Richard J. Aronson	Economics	Lehigh University
Eugen Baer	Philosophy	Hobart & Wm. Smith Colleges
Albert Bandura	Psychology	Stanford University
Geoffrey Barraclough	History	Brandeis University
Eric Beukenkamp	Applied Linguistics	Cornell University
Tessa Blackstone	Sociology	University of London, London, England
Colin Blakemore	Psychology	Oxford University, Oxford, England
Paul Bohannon	Anthropology	University of California at Santa Barbara
George Bozzini	Applied Linguistics	George Washington University
William R. Breneman	Biology	Indiana University
Edward H. Buehrig	Political Science	Indiana University

Robert F. Byrnes	History	Indiana University
Lynton K. Caldwell	Political Science	Indiana University
Gordon Cameron	Urban Planning	Cambridge University, Cambridge, England
Kay Carmichael	Social Administration	University of Glasgow, Glasgow, Scotland
John Cochran	Economics	Arizona State University
Bernard I. Cohen	History of Science	Harvard University
William Condon	Psychiatry	Boston University
Sir Alan Cottrell	Physics	Cambridge University, Cambridge, England
Lawrence A. Cremin	History	Teachers College, Columbia University
Ivor Davies	Instructional Systems Technology	Indiana University
Luis Davila	Chicano-Riqueno Studies	Indiana University
W. Jackson Davis	Biology and Psychobiology	University of California at Santa Cruz
Bruno DeFinetti	Mathematics	University of Rome (Emeritus), Rome, Italy
Henri Dieuzeide	Structures, Methods, and Techniques of Education	Unesco, Paris, France
Hughes de Jouvenel	Law	Association Internationale Futuribles, Paris, France
Harold C. Dent	History of Education	University of London (Emeritus) East Sussex, England
Ricardo Diez-Hochleitner	Social Work	Fundación General Mediterrânea, Madrid, Spain
Leroy Eyring	Chemistry	Arizona State University
Robert H. Ferrell	History	Indiana University
Judith R. Franz	Physics	Indiana University
Jacob Fuchs	Chemistry	Arizona State University

Paul H. Gebhard	Anthropology	Indiana University
Alexander L. George	Political Science	Stanford University
William Gray	Administration	Strathelyde Educational Authority, Glasgow, Scotland
Nelson George Hairston	Zoology	University of North Carolina
Edward T. Hall	Anthropology	Northwestern University (Emeritus)
John A. Hamilton	Medicine	University of Glasgow, Glasgow, Scotland
Norman Hanshey	Futures Studies	McGill University, Montreal, Quebec
Walter Heller	Economics	University of Minnesota
Henry Hinke	Political Science	Arizona State University
Robert Hirt	Religion	Rabbi Isaac Elchanan Theological Seminary, New York, New York
Earl Hopper	Sociology	University of London, London, England
Thomas Ford Hoult	Sociology	Arizona State University
Teo Lye Huay	Administration	Gan Eng Seng Secondary School, Singapore
Paul Hubbard	History	Arizona State University
John Hudson	Sociology	Arizona State University
L. C. Hunter	Economic Research	University of Glasgow, Glasgow, Scotland
Torsten Husén	International Education	University of Stockholm, Stockholm, Sweden
Charles S. Hyneman	Political Science	Indiana University
Richard H. Jahns	Earth Sciences	Stanford University
B. K. Yogini Janki	Spiritual Education	Spiritual University, Rajasthan, India
Henri Janne	Sociology	Free University of Brussels, Brussels, Belgium
William Kenan Jr.	Physics	University of North Carolina
Alexander King	Law	Association Internationale Futuribles, Paris, France

Boris Kluchnikov	Economics	Unesco, Paris, France (on leave from Moscow University)
E. R. Laithwaite	Science and Technology	Imperial College, London, England
D. Latouche	Political Science	McGill University, Montreal, Quebec
Leonard H. Leigh	Criminology	London School of Economics, London, England
Sutichai Liangjayetz	Personnel	Office of Higher Education, Bangkok, Thailand
Donald Lichtenberg	Physics	Oxford University, Oxford, England (on leave from Indiana University)
Fred Lindstrom	Sociology	Arizona State University
James Ross MacDonald	Physics	University of North Carolina
Malcolm Mackenzie	Education	University of Glasgow, Glasgow, Scotland
Douglas H. H. McNaughton	Religion	Auchingramont Presbyterian Church, Hamilton, Scotland
Duncan Macrae, Jr.	Political Science and Sociology	University of North Carolina
Fritz Machlup	Economics	Princeton University
Henry R. Mahler	Chemistry	Indiana University
Michael Marien	Sociology	Information for Policy Design, Lafayette, New York
Martin E. Marty	Religion	University of Chicago Divinity School
Eleanora Masini	Social Science	Pontificial Gregoriana University, Rome, Prati, Italy
James V. McConnell	Psychology	University of Michigan
Vincent E. McKelvey	Geology	U.S. Geological Survey (retired), Reston, Virginia
William H. McNeill	History	University of Chicago
George McRobie	Physics	Intermediate Technological Development Group Ltd., London, England
John F. Mee	Business	Indiana University
Howard Mehlinger	Social Sciences	Indiana University

Lynne Merritt	Chemistry	Indiana University
Delbert C. Miller	Sociology	Indiana University
Rita Levi Montaleini	Sociology	University of Madrid, Madrid, Spain
Sir Nevill F. Mott	Physics	Cambridge University, Cambridge, England
Robert Muller	Economic and Social Council	United Nations, New York, New York
Haydn H. Murray	Geology	Indiana University
Henri Nouwen	Religion	Yale University Divinity School
Elizabeth T. Odum	Biology	Sante Fe Community College, Gainesville, Florida
Lindsay S. Olive	Botany	University of North Carolina
Yee Sze Onn	Social Sciences	Institute of Education, Singapore
Leon Pacala	Religion	Colgate-Rochester Seminary, Rochester, New York
Vance Packard	Social Commentator	New Canaan, Connecticut
Charles F. Park Jr.	Geo-sciences	Stanford University
George A. Parks	Earth Science	Stanford University
John B. Patton	Geology	Indiana University
Aurelio Peccei	Law	Club of Rome, Rome, Italy
John Platt	Biophysics	Boston University School of Medicine
Guy Poquét	Research	Association Internationale Futuribles, Paris, France
John J. W. Rogers	Geology	University of North Carolina
Roy Radha	Physics	Arizona State University
Reynold Ruppe	Anthropology	Arizona State University
Sally Swing Shelley	Non-governmental Organization Section	United Nations, New York, New York
Robert St. Clair	Linguistics	University of Louisville
Anthony G. San Pietro	Plant Bio-chemistry	Indiana University

Joseph J. Schwab	Education	Center for the Study of Democratic Institutions, Berkeley, California
Thomas A. Sebeok	Language and Semiotic Studies	Indiana University
Walter H. C. Simmonds	Policy Analyst	National Research Council of Canada, Ottawa, Ontario
Brian J. Skinner	Geology and Geophysics	Yale University
Gary A. Sojka	Biology	Indiana University
Tracy M. Sonneborn	Zoology	Indiana University (Emeritus)
Song Sak Srikalasin	Academic Affairs	Sri Nakharinwirot University, Bangkok, Thailand
Shona Tropp	Administration	Unesco, Paris, France
Kimon Valaskakis	Economics	University of Montreal, Montreal, Quebec
Roberto Vacca	Systems Research	Consultant to Italian Regional Governments, Rome, Italy
George Vaideanu	Structures, Methods, and Techniques of Education	Unesco, Paris, France
Sir Geoffrey Vickers	Law and Economics	The Grange, Goring-on-Thames, England
Aldo Visalberghi	Education	University of Rome, Rome, Italy
Raymond E. Wanner	Government	Unesco, Paris, France
Lawrence Leslie Waters	Transportation and Business History	Indiana University
Willem Welling	Administration	Van Leer Foundation, The Hague, Netherlands
Richard Samuel Westfall	History and Philosophy of Science	Indiana University
Suthichai Wiengjayetz	Personnel Administration	Office of Higher Education, Bangkok, Thailand
Peter Wilby	Social Journalism	London Times, London, England

Eric Wilkerson	Education	University of Glasgow, Glasgow, Scotland
York Y. Willbern	Political Science	Indiana University
Eryl Hall Williams	Criminology	London School of Economics, London, England
E. O. Wilson	Science	Harvard University
George W. Wilson	Business Administration	Indiana University
Lawrence Wylie	French Civilization	Harvard University
O. L. Zangwill	Experimental Psychology	Cambridge University, Cambridge, England

Appendix C*
Bibliography of General Interest from the Natural and Social Sciences

The publications listed in this bibliography have been suggested by the panel of scholars who participated in this study. The titles listed will introduce the reader to some of the major concepts from each of the disciplines included in this study.

Bandura, Albert. "Self Referent Thought: The Development of Self-Efficacy." In *Development of Social Cognition*, edited by J. H. Flavell and L. D. Ross, forthcoming.

Barraclough, Geoffrey. "Universal History." In *Approaches to History, A Symposium*, edited by H. P. R. Finberg. Toronto: University of Toronto Press, 1962.

Blakemore, Colin. *Mechanics of the Mind*. Cambridge, Cambridge University Press, 1977.

Caldwell, Lynton K. "Biology and Bureaucracy: The Coming Confrontation." *Public Administration Review*, January-February 1980, pp. 1-12.

Caldwell, Lynton K. "Human Limitations and the Future of Technology." *Humanitas* (Journal of the Institute of Man) 14 (1978): 47-60.

Caldwell, Lynton K. "1992: Threshold to the Postmodern World." *A Time To Hear and Answer: Essays for the Bicentennial Season. The Franklin Lectures in the Sciences and the Humanities*. Fourth Series. University, Alabama: University of Alabama Press for Auburn University, 1977.

Cochran, John A. *Money, Banking, and the Economy*. 4th ed. New York: The Macmillan Company, 1979.

Cohen, I. Bernard. *The Birth of a New Physics*. Garden City, N.Y.: Anchor Books, 1960.

Cook, Earl. "Limits to Exploitation of Nonrenewable Resources." *Materials: Renewable and Nonrenewable Resources*. No. 4, Science Special Compendia.

Crick, Francis. "Split Genes and RNA Splicing." *Science* 204 (1979): 264.

*Also see Appendix D which includes a number of natural and social science publications with a direct linkage to the future.

Diez-Hochleitner, Ricardo. *The Spanish Educational Reform and Lifelong Education.* Paris: International Bureau of Education and Unesco Institute for Education, 1978.

Dobzhansky, Theodosius. *Genetic Diversity and Human Equality.* New York,: Basic Books, 1973.

Gillespie, Charles. *The Edge of Objectivity: An Essay in the History of Scientific Ideas.* Princeton, N.J.: Princeton University Press, 1960.

Hall, Edward T. *Beyond Culture.* New York: Doubleday, 1977.

Handler, Philip. ed. *Biology and the Future of Man.* New York: Oxford University Press, 1970.

Hopper, Earl. *Social Mobility: A Study of Social Control and Insatiability,* forthcoming.

Hoult, Thomas Ford. "The Humanist Perspective." In *Theoretical Perspectives in Sociology,* edited by Scott G. McNall. New York: St. Martin's Press, 1979, pp. 83-95.

Husên, Torsten. *The School in Question.* London and New York: Oxford University Press, 1979.

Ivensen, Leslie L. "The Chemistry of the Brain." *Scientific American* 24 (1979): 134 ff.

Judson, Horace F. *The Eighth Day of Creation.* New York: Simon and Schuster, 1979.

Kuhn, Thomas S. *The Structure of Scientific Revolutions.* 2nd ed. Chicago: University of Chicago Press, 1970.

McConnell, James V. *Understanding Human Behavior.* 3rd ed. New York: Holt, Rinehart and Winston, Inc., 1980.

McNeill, W. H. *The Rise of the West: A History of the Human Community.* Chicago: University of Chicago Press, 1963.

McRobie, George and Carr, M. "Mass Production or Production for the Masses? Technology: A Critical Choice for Developing Countries." In *Dynamics of Development,* edited by S. K. Sharma, New Delhi: Concept Library, 1977.

Marien, Michael. "Toward a Devolution of Services." *Social Policy* 9 (1978): 26-35.

Marsden, R. W., ed. *Politics, Minerals, and Survival.* Madison: University of Wisconsin Press, 1974.

Matthews, S. W. "This Changing Earth." *National Geographic* 143 (1973): 1.

Monod, Jacques. *Chance and Necessity: An Essay on the Natural Philosophy of Modern Biology.* New York: Knopf, 1971.

Mott, Sir Nevill. "Theory and Experiment Since Schrodinger's Equation." *Physics Bulletin* 25 (1974): 448-451.

Odum, Howard T. *Environment, Power and Society.* New York: John Wiley, Interscience, 1971.

Odum, Howard T. and Elizabeth C. *Energy: Basis for Man and Nature.* New York: McGraw-Hill Book Company, 1976.

Park, Charles F., Jr. *Affluence in Jeopardy: Minerals and the Political Economy.* San Francisco: Freeman, Cooper and Co., 1968.

Patton, John B. "The Invisible Crisis: Implications of Federal Energy Policy." *The Review* 20 (1978): 13-22.

Peccei, Aurelio. *The Human Quality.* Oxford: Pergamon Press, 1977.

Platt, John. "Lock-Ins and Multiple Lock-Ins in Collective Behavior." *American Scientist* 57 (1969): 96-100.

Platt, John. "Social Traps." *American Psychologist* 28 (1969): 641-651.
Platt, John. "What We Must Do." *Science* 166 (1969): 115-121.
Polya, George. *How to Solve It: A New Aspect of Mathematical Method.* 2nd ed. Princeton: Princeton University Press, 1971.
Schumacher, Ernst F. *Small is Beautiful: Economics as if People Mattered.* New York: Harper and Row, 1973.
"Economic Development." *Scientific American* 243 (1980): 3. (entire issue)
Steward, Julian. *Theory of Culture Change.* Urbana, Illinois: University of Illinois Press, 1955.
Valaskakis, Kimon. *The Information Society: The Issue and the Choices.* A report on the Gamma Information Society Project, University of Montreal, 1979.
Vickers, Geoffrey. "Equality of Responsibility." *Futures,* February 1979, p. 16-31.
Vickers, Geoffrey. "The Future of Morality." *Futures,* October 1979, pp. 371-382.
Vickers, Geoffrey. "Reshaping Western Culture." *Futures,* December, 1977, p. 457.
Weizenbaum, Joseph. *Computer Power and Human Reason.* San Francisco: W. H. Freeman and Company, 1976.

Appendix D

Selected Background Readings With Implications For Educational Change

Any selected bibliography is a reflection of preferences and prejudices. This bibliography, culled from a list of over 1200 titles, is heavily weighted toward educational futures and futures studies. For example, Edward Cornish's *The Study of the Future*, would be very useful to persons interested in the future and its educational implications. Other books are more difficult to categorize, such as Alvin Toffler's *The Third Wave*, Lester Brown's *The Twenty-Ninth Day*, W. Jackson Davis's *The Seventh Year*, or Garrett Hardin's *Promethean Ethics*. These books deal with the study of the future but are predominantly concerned with the social and the natural sciences rather than with education per se. With a few exceptions, the numerous books and articles listed in the footnotes are not duplicated in this bibliography. We hope this selected bibliography will prove useful to those just beginning to study the future as well as to those with sophistication in the field.

Andrews, Frank M., and Withey, Stephen B. *Social Indicators of Well-Being in America: The Development and Measurement of Perceptual Indicators*. New York: Plenum Publishers, 1976.

Ayres, Robert V. *Technological Forecasting and Long-Range Planning*. New York: Holt, Rinehart and Winston, Inc., 1971.

Bahm, A. J. *The Philosopher's World Model*. Westport, Conn.: Greenwood Press, 1979.

Bell, Daniel. *The Coming of the Post-Industrial Society: A Venture in Social Forecasting*. New York: Basic Books, 1972.

Bezold, Clement, ed. *Anticipatory Democracy: People in the Politics of the Future*. New York: Vintage Books, 1978.

Bizien, Yves. *Population and Economic Development*. New York: Praeger, 1979.

Bookchin, Murray. *The Limits of the City*. New York: Harper and Row, 1974.

Botkin, James W.; Mahdi, Elmandjra; and Malitza, Mircea. *No Limits to Learning: Bridging the Human Gap*. Elmsford, N.Y.: Pergamon Press, 1979.

Boucher, Wayne I., ed. *The Study of the Future: An Agenda for Research.* Washington, D.C.: U.S. Government Printing Office, 1977.
Boulding, Elise. *The Underside of History: A View of Women Through Time.* Boulder, Colo.: Westview Press, 1977.
Boulding, Kenneth. *From Abundance to Scarcity: Implications for the American Tradition.* Columbus, Ohio: Ohio State University Press, 1977.
Boulding, Kenneth. *The Social System of the Planet Earth.* Reading, Mass.: Addison-Wesley, 1977.
Brameld, Theodore. *The Teacher as World Citizen—A Scenario of the 21st Century.* Homewood, Ill.: ETC Publications, 1975.
Brown, Lester. *Resource Trends and Population: A Time for Reassessment.* Washington, D.C.: Worldwatch Institute, Paper 29, May 1979.
Brown, Lester. *The Twenty-Ninth Day.* New York: W. W. Norton, 1978.
Carnegie Commission. *A Public Trust: The Report of the Carnegie Commission on the Future of Public Broadcasting.* New York: Bantam Books, 1979.
Cellarius, Richard A., and Platt, John. "Councils of Urgent Studies." *Science* 177 (1972): 670-676.
Commoner, Barry. *The Politics of Energy.* New York: Alfred A. Knopf, 1979.
Cornish, Edward. *The Study of the Future.* Washington, D.C.: World Future Society, 1977.
Davis, W. Jackson. *The Seventh Year.* New York: W. W. Norton, 1979.
deChardin, Teilhard. *The Future of Man.* London: William Collins Sons & Co., Ltd., 1959.
Dolman, Anthony, and Tinbergen, Jan, eds. *Reshaping the International Order: A Report to the Club of Rome.* New York: E. P. Dutton, 1976.
Dror, Yehezkel. *Crazy States: A Counterconventional Strategic Problem.* Millwood, N.Y.: Kraus-Thomson Organization, 1980.
Ebel, Roland H. "Get Ready for the L-Bomb: A Preliminary Social Assessment of Longevity Technology." *Technological Forecasting and Social Change* 13 (1979): 131-148.
"Economic Development." *Scientific American* 243 (1980): 3. (entire issue)
Ehrlich, Paul. *The Population Bomb.* Mattituck, New York: American Reprint Co./Rivercity Press, 1975.
Evans, Christopher. *The Micromillennium.* New York: The Viking Press, 1979.
"The Exploration of the Future." *Realities* (1966): 50-58.
Feather, Frank. *Through the '80s: Thinking Globally, Acting Locally.* Washington, D.C.: World Future Society, 1980.
Franko, L. G., and Seiber, Marilyn J. *Developing Country Debt.* New York: Pergamon Press, 1979.
Fowles, Jib, ed. *Handbook of Future Research.* Westport, Conn.: Greenwood Press, 1978.
Fromm, Erich. *To Have Or To Be.* World Perspective Series. New York: Harper and row, 1976.
Fuhrmann, Ernst. "The Longlife Car." *Futures* 11 (1979): 216-223.
Gabor, Dennis. *The Mature Society.* New York: Praeger Publishers, 1972.
Galbraith, John Kenneth. *The Age of Uncertainty.* Boston: Houghton Mifflin, 1977.
Gappert, Gary. *Post-Affluent America: The Social Economy of the Future.* New York: Franklin Watts, 1979.

Hafele, Wolf, and Sassin, Wolfgang. "The Global Energy System." *Behavioral Science* 24 (1979): 169-189.
Hall, Edward T. *The Hidden Dimension.* Garden City, N.Y.: Doubleday, 1966.
Hardin, Garrett. *Promethean Ethics.* Seattle: University of Washington Press, 1980.
Hardin, Garrett. "The Tragedy of the Commons." *Science*, 13 December 1968, pp. 1243-1248.
Heilbroner, Robert. *An Inquiry Into the Human Prospect.* New York: W. W. Norton, Inc., 1974.
Higgins, Ronald. "The Seventh Enemy: The Human Factor in the Global Crisis." *The New Ecologist* 9 (1979): 6-10.
Hudson Institute Study. *The Corporate Environment, 1975-1985.* Croton-on-Hudson, N.Y.: Hudson Institute, 1971.
Jameson, Kenneth P., and Wilber, Charles K. *Directions in Economic Development.* South Bend, Ind.: University of Notre Dame Press, 1979.
Jungk, Robert. *Millennial Man: A World Report on the Prospects for a Humane Future.* New York: Liveright, 1976.
Jones, Thomas E. *Options for the Future.* New York, N.Y.: Praeger, 1980.
Kahn, Herman. *The Next Two Hundred Years.* New York: Morrow, 1976.
Kahn, Herman. *World Economic Development: 1979 and Beyond.* Boulder, Co.: Westview Press, 1979.
Kohr, Leopold. *The Overdeveloped Nations: The Diseconomies of Scale.* New York: Schocken Books, 1978.
Laslo, Ervin, ed. *Goals of Mankind: A Report to the Club of Rome on the New Horizons of Global Community.* New York: Dutton, 1977.
Legum, Colin. *Africa in the 1980s: A Continent in Crisis.* New York: McGraw-Hill, 1979.
"Les Savants Scrutent L'Avenir." *Realities* 237 (1965): 106-111.
Mead, Margaret. *World Enough: Rethinking the Future.* Boston, Mass.: Little, Brown, 1976.
Mesarovic, Mihajlo and Pestel, Eduard. *Mankind at the Turning Point: The Second Report to the Club of Rome.* New York: Reader's Digest Press/Dutton, 1974.
Michael, Donald N. "L'Avenir du Temps Libré." *Economie Et Humanisme* 167 (1966): 3-12.
Newland, Kathleen. *The Sisterhood of Man.* New York: W. W. Norton, 1979.
Orlosky, Donald E. and Smith, B. Othanel. *Curriculum Development: Issues And Insights.* Chicago: Rand McNally College Publishing Company, 1978.
Orr, David W. "Catastrophe and Social Order." *Human Ecology* 7 (1979): 41-52.
Pascarella, Perry. *Technology: Fire in a Dark World.* New York: Van Nostrand-Reinhold, 1979.
Peterson, R. E. *Lifelong Learning in America.* San Francisco: Jossey-Bass, Inc., 1979.
Platt, John. "What We Must Do." *Science* 166 (1969): 1115-1121.
Pollock, John C. *The Politics of Crisis Reporting: American Journalism and Foreign Affairs.* New York: Praeger, 1979.
Robertson, A. H. "The Outlook for Social Security." *The American Economic Review* 69 (1979): 272-274.

Roszak, Theodore. *Person/Planet: The Creative Disintegration of Industrial Society*. New York: Anchor Press, 1978.
Rubin, Louis, ed. *The Future of Education: Perspective on Tomorrow's Schooling*. Boston: Allyn and Bacon, 1975.
Salk, Jonas. *The Survival of the Wisest*. New York: Harper and Row, 1973.
Shane, Harold G. "America's Educational Futures: 1976-2001: The Views of 50 Distinguished World Citizens and Educators." *The Futurist* 10 (1976): 252-257.
Shane, Harold G. *Curriculum Change Toward the 21st Century*. Washington, D.C.: The National Education Association, 1977.
Shane, Harold G. *The Educational Significance of the Future*. Bloomington, Indiana: Phi Delta Kappa, 1973.
Shane, Harold G. "Looking to the Future: Reassessment of Educational Issues of the 1970's." *Phi Delta Kappan* 54 (1973): 326-337.
Simon, Julian L. "Resources, Environment, Population: An Oversupply of False Bad News." *Science* 208 (1980): 1431-1437.
Spekke, Andrew A. *The Next 25 Years: Crisis and Opportunity*. Washington, D.C.: World Future Society, 1975.
Thurow, Lester C. *The Zero-Sum Society*. New York: Basic Books, 1980.
Toffler, Alvin. *The Ecospasm Report*. New York: Bantam Books, 1975.
Toffler, Alvin. *The Third Wave*. New York: William Morrow, 1980.
Tyrwhitt, J. "The Child in the World of Tomorrow." *Ekistics* 272 (1978): 335-403.
UNESCO. *Suicide or Survival? The Challenge of the Year 2000*. Paris: Unesco, December, 1978.
Valaskakis, Kimon. *The Conserver Society: A Workable Alternative for the Future*. New York: Harper and Row, 1979.
Waddington, D. H. Ciba Foundation Symposium #36. *The Future as an Academic Discipline*. Amsterdam, Netherlands: Elsevier/Excerpta Medica/North-Holland, 1975.